Costume Society of America series

Phyllis A. Specht, Series Editor

DRESSING MODERN MATERNITY

The Frankfurt Sisters of Dallas and the Page Boy Label

To Anna
Enjoy
Kay Goldman
September 2013

KAY GOLDMAN

Texas Tech University Press

Designed by Kasey McBeath
Jacket photos: Maternity fashions by Page Boy shown February 18, 1947, and June 17, 1957. Courtesy the Frankfurt Family Collection.

This book is catalogued with the Library of Congress.
ISBN (cloth): 978-0-89672-799-1
ISBN (e-book): 978-0-89672-809-7

Printed in the United States of America
13 14 15 16 17 18 19 20 21 / 9 8 7 6 5 4 3 2 1

Texas Tech University Press
Box 41037 | Lubbock, Texas 79409-1037 USA
800.832.4042 | ttup@ttu.edu | www.ttupress.org

This work is dedicated to three remarkable women: Edna Frankfurt Ravkind, Elsie Frankfurt Pollock, and Louise Frankfurt Gartner, who envisioned the idea that became Page Boy Maternity Company. Without their inspiring work, there would be no story to tell. It is also dedicated to the Jewish women of earlier generations who believed enough in themselves to break down barriers and become businesswomen. They refused to be limited by naysayers. They made it easier for those of us who came later to dream and, by dreaming, to achieve.

Contents

Illustrations

Acknowledgments

owe a profound debt to many people who helped me bring this remarkable story to life. My mother told me the story about three Jewish sisters she knew when she was growing up in Dallas during the 1930s. She described their accomplishments, explaining to me that they had been granted a patent for their unique design that became the first real maternity dress—a dress that made pregnant women look fashionable. Without her story in the back of my memory, I would never have started this project.

My editors have been amazingly supportive. First I would not have imagined turning my short presentation into a book without the encouragement and support of Judith Keeling. She and Joanna Conrad were ever ready to answer my questions and allay my uncertainties.

I also owe much to members of the Gartner, Pollock, and Ravkind families, who shared their memories about the Frankfurt sisters, were willing to answer my incessant questions, and made copies of photographs for me. I want to especially thank Gigi Gartner, who coordinated my interview with her mother, Louise Frankfurt Gartner, and her mother Louise, who graciously allowed me to visit her in her home. Furthermore I am immeasurably indebted to Penny Pollock, who made it possible for me to have in my possession the wonderful scrapbooks kept by her stepmother, Elsie Frankfurt Pollock, and for providing information about the last years of Page Boy's existence. Other family members also willingly shared their memories with me: these include Brenda Berg, Joan Susman, and Morris Weiss.

I was able to add details to this story because I received help from many librarians. I want to especially thank my friend Bill Page from Evans Library at Texas A&M, who is always willing to assist me and is continually on the lookout for information he believes I can use. I also had assistance from other Texas A&M librarians: Anne Patterson, from the West Campus Library; Laura Sare, Government Information Librarian; and Joel Thornton, Business Librarian. I also want to thank Edward Hoyenski, Collection Manager, Texas Fashion Collection at the University of North Texas. Without his help I would not have uncovered the wonderful Kennedy dress. I also had help from Marianne Martin from Colonial Williamsburg Foundation, Debra Hughes, and Linda Gross from Hagley Museum and Library.

Finally, I want to thank my fantastic daughter, Dorie Goldman, who helped me focus my thoughts when my writing wandered and generously agreed to be my first reader.

DRESSING MODERN MATERNITY

Introduction

n 1938 two optimistic young women gathered together $500 and began a new business: designing and manufacturing maternity clothing.[1] Within a few years the business, Page Boy Maternity Clothing, became the foremost maternity clothing manufacturing concern in the United States. Page Boy's phenomenal growth also enabled a Dallas, Texas, entrepreneur to become the first woman inducted into the Young Presidents' Organization and led to the firm's recognition as an innovator in marketing and clothing design.

Elsie Frankfurt, along with her sisters Edna and Louise, turned a revolutionary idea into a novel and successful manufacturing venture. The success of the business, Page Boy Maternity Corporation, was based on an innovative design that allowed a maternity skirt to fit snugly around the hips while making allowances for an expanding abdomen. This design prevented the skirt from hiking up in the front. Previous maternity dresses often rose up over the abdomen making the skirt front appear shorter than the sides and back. Dressmakers had not been able to solve the challenge of the short skirt, but Elsie Frankfurt was able to overcome this problem. Elsie's design, based on engineering principles she had learned in her design classes, earned her and her sister Edna a patent.

The mere fact that Elsie and Edna considered obtaining a patent is remarkable. Although Edna worked as an executive secretary for an oil company and Elsie had earned a college degree, these young women were not sophisticated entrepreneurs who had set out to revolutionize the maternity fashion world or any other business. Nevertheless, once they had the design they realized that it needed to be protected by a patent, and with that step of patenting their design, they joined a small group of innovative women who had previously applied for and been granted patents.

United States patent law originated from the Constitution, and the first patent act was passed by Congress in 1790. United States patent regulations recognize three main types of patents: utility, design, and plant. The utility patents are typically machines or items of use. Design patents are items like Elsie's skirt, or a particular patented design for the shape of a bottle, or some other useful item. The plant patent was granted for the asexual reproduction of new plants such as hybrids. Although the patent office does not keep records of the gender of those who receive patents, patent office records indicate that the first woman to be granted a patent was Mary Kies, who earned a patent for "straw weaving with silk thread." That patent was issued on May 5, 1808.

Based on a study done by the U.S. patent office, 5,535 patents were granted to women between the years of 1790 and 1895. This number represented about 1 percent of the total patents issued during those years. Another calculation indicates that between 1790 and 1985 about 1.5 percent of U. S. patents were granted to women, and still another study indicates that between 1890 and about 1950 about 1.4 percent of patents were granted to women. In 1937 the patent office granted 5,137 design patents. Although no specific information exists about the number of women who received patents that year, several studies suggest that between 1.4 and 1.5 percent of patents were issued to women. Thus, an esti-

mate would put the number of women who earned patents for their designs in 1937 at between 71 and 77.[2] Edna and Elsie were probably among fewer than 100 women who were granted patents in 1937.

The patent that protected Elsie and Edna's design from others who might have copied the style set the stage for their remarkable success. The sisters also created a model business plan for themselves that worked for several decades. During those years Page Boy and the Frankfurt sisters became national figures. During the two decades after World War II, the average family income was increasing almost continually at a rate of 4–5 percent per year. However, Page Boy failed to grasp both the importance of this growth to consumer buying power and the magnitude of the change it would bring to consumption habits. Eventually Page Boy lost the momentum to grow.[3]

In the beginning the sisters never set out to become the preeminent maternity fashion house of the 1940s, '50s, and '60s. However, their gift for design and their innate management style created a successful business. Moreover, the fact that they were women gave them an advantage that other manufacturers found difficult to overcome. The sisters were tightfisted with their own funds—never paying for something they could get for free. For example, after World War II, the sisters became adept at obtaining free publicity. The uniqueness of the business brought journalists to their offices. After all, what better copy could a magazine or newspapers want than a story about three smart, attractive, young women? And after several Hollywood stars bought Page Boy wardrobes, Elsie learned to take advantage of the famous names: she always revealed which stars had shopped in their stores. She used photographs of these women in promotional copy, and she was an inveterate name dropper.

Edna, Elsie, and Louise learned to save in other ways. For example, Elsie offered to write a fashion column for the Dallas paper—putting her name and the Page Boy label in the paper without having to purchase advertising space. Similarly, they used friends as advertisements and sales representatives. If a pregnant friend was visiting family in another town or state, the friend often called on the local department stores wearing one of Elsie or Louise's designs. These women even took orders for the company, and it never hurt that many of the department stores across the South were owned by Jewish merchants or that the owners might be acquainted with the visiting woman.

Finally, the sisters stretched every dime and penny earned in their business because they knew how to play the game, and as women they stood out at business events. For instance, they not only got free publicity but also got free lunches when they dined at the weekly fashion shows held at the Statler Hotel in downtown Dallas. One trick they used worked like this: They ate lunch at the hotel, as did many businessmen. Most weeks one businessman or even several would offer to pay for their lunch. But if no one offered to pay, the sisters would fumble in their purses, looking for money; because they purposefully never carried cash, they could not pay. Seeing their predicament, one of the gentlemen would always come to their rescue and pay their tab.

Although the sisters never created any long-range business plans, the business thrived because of Edna and Elsie's shrewd business instincts and Louise's flair for creative design and fashion. One of the most significant decisions they made was selecting the location for their first retail shop. Elsie and Edna picked the perfect spot and rented space in the Medical Arts Building in Dallas. This building housed the offices of many obstetricians, and the first-floor location forced women to walk past the Page Boy windows on their way to their appointments. During World War II, Page Boy managed to continue manufacturing and selling maternity clothes—despite severe war restrictions. Originally, Page Boy's first outfits were sold as suites and priced for the upscale market, but as the war progressed Page Boy changed its operation. War restrictions prevented two garments from being sold together, so Page Boy priced the items individually. The sisters learned from this experience and continued to sell some items as separates after the war. But despite war limitations on fabric and rules preventing manufacturers from taking on new customers, Page Boy's financial situation strengthened, and they came out of the war ready to expand.

During the early decades of the business, each sister worked full time in the business and they rarely hired nonfamily administrators. Even when they did hire outsiders, those employees remained employees, and Elsie and Edna never allowed them major decision-making power or a share in the company. Furthermore, like many Americans reared during the Depression, the women rarely purchased anything for which they could not pay cash, but in the end this frugal philosophy stifled the growth of their business, and these two business theories came to haunt the final year of the firm.

The sisters were innovators in other ways also. In the 1940s and 1950s, when manufacturers often sold their products through jobbers,[4] who represented the manufacturers and sold the manufacturers' goods to local department stores, as opposed to selling their own products in their own shops, Page Boy opened its own retail outlets as well as selling directly to department stores. Furthermore, the sisters never used jobbers. Perhaps they felt they wanted to have more personal involvement with the customers, whether the customers were individual women or department stores. But several decades later, when other name brand manufacturers began opening their own shops in malls across the country, Page Boy failed to expand the number of outlets it owned and failed to grasp the importance of accessibility and visibility of its brand to new customers. The customers moved into the suburbs and beyond, but Page Boy never accommodated this change. Perhaps these failures were rooted in the sisters' age and lack of outside influence. Neither of the sisters who remained active in the business lived in the suburbs, and they failed to grasp the importance of having a nearby shop.

Edna and Elsie were individuals born as the twentieth century began—before World War I—and Louise was born shortly after the war ended. At that time in Texas, transportation between most small communities was difficult. Families relied on horses and buggies or even rode individually on horseback to get from place to place or from railroad stops to other cities not on the rail line. When automobiles became available their use was often limited to in-town travel since Texas roads were poor and often impassible. Modern amenities, such as gas lighting and later electric lights, running water, and sewage disposal, became available in the larger cities such as Galveston, Dallas, Houston, and Waco but not in the smaller towns. The Frankfurt sisters were born in an unhurried era of measured development and slow change.

The young women who established Page Boy were first-generation Texas Jews. Both of their parents, Benjamin Frankfurt and Jenny Bergman, had emigrated from Eastern Europe. As immigrants they were members of families who willingly left behind the enveloping society of Eastern European Jewish culture. These families arrived in the United States seeking new opportunities; however, they also faced a completely alien culture. In all likelihood the families suffered some forms of oppression in Eastern Europe from which they could escape by making this trip to America. American culture encouraged assimilation rather than separation and alienation, and both Benjamin Frankfurt and Jenny Bergman's families voluntarily embraced the unfamiliar. The way these families responded to the challenges of the new society contributed to their assimilation: they settled neither in New York nor along the East Coast where millions of fellow Eastern European Jews had put down roots. Instead they embraced the American spirit of pioneering and moved west. By 1900 Jenny Bergman's family resided in St. Louis, Missouri, where her father, or perhaps her stepfather, worked as a tailor and her older sister worked as a seamstress.[5] Jenny herself worked as a cook.

Shortly after arriving in the United States, immigrant Benjamin Frankfurt settled in Cushing, Texas, a newly incorporated town along the rail line in the Piney Woods of East Texas. Cushing, a small community near the old colonial settlement of Nacogdoches, never became prosperous like some other railroad stops, but it was in this setting that Benjamin learned about American economic opportunities.

Benjamin, like many other Jewish immigrants, opened a small mercantile store selling a variety of goods. Family members remember Ben saying that he never made much money while he was living in Cushing. In fact, he was so impoverished that he only purchased a few items at a time—never actually fully stocking his shelves but leaving many of them empty. To hide the bare shelves, he hung curtains along the ceiling that hung down, covering the shelves. He only pulled back small sections of the curtains when someone came in to make a purchase, never exposing the bare shelves.[6]

Although the family does not know how Jenny and Benjamin met, the two young people were married in St. Louis on March 10, 1906, and after the wedding they returned to Texas. Once the railroad extended past Cushing, Benjamin probably realized that the town was never going to prosper, and by 1910, he had moved the family to Athens, Texas, about seventy miles northwest of Cushing. Benjamin was now the proprietor of a more successful business, and Jenny had given birth to two children, Edna and Victor.[7]

During the next decade Ben's business improved, and he and his family were able to travel back and forth to St. Louis to visit Jenny's family. Ben even patronized the Dallas Trade League shows so that he could examine the latest manufactured goods and socialize with other merchants. In 1909 he visited Dallas along with other businessmen who placed their orders with Dallas jobbers. Four years later business reports in the newspaper mentioned that he was one of the visiting merchants who shopped at the wholesale houses during the Fall Trade Excursion.[8] Since his name was reported in the paper, he was probably familiar to the Dallas merchants and wholesalers.

When World War I threatened to engulf the United States, Ben took his wife and children back to St. Louis, where in September of 1918 he registered for the draft. By this time he was nearly thirty years old. On his draft card he listed his occupation as self-employed shoe merchant; he did not open a dry-goods or mercantile shop but instead decided that in

St. Louis he would open a specialty shop. Within a few years he was back in Texas, but he had given up small-town life. By 1920 Ben had settled in Dallas, a place with a growing Jewish population and expanding business opportunities. Now living in the big city, he abandoned merchandising and began dealing in real estate—a profession well suited to his gregarious personality.

This move allowed the family to experience a different cultural environment than they had experienced while living in Cushing and Athens. Ben and Jenny were most likely the only Jewish citizens living in Cushing, and although Athens probably had other Jewish merchants, the community never established a Jewish cemetery, and the nearest town with a Jewish congregation was Corsicana, about thirty-five miles away. During the early decades of the twentieth century, traveling even thirty-five miles with several small children would be a hardship. When they moved to Dallas, Ben, Jenny, and the family first settled in Oak Cliff on the south side of the Trinity River. Within a few years Jenny decided they should move to South Dallas, a section with many other Jewish families and an area with several Jewish congregations. Without telling her husband, Jenny rented an apartment in South Dallas and announced that she planned to move so that her children could socialize with other Jewish teens.[9] So the family moved.

According to Gigi Gartner, Ben's granddaughter, Ben was determined to observe Orthodox Jewish traditions after he moved to Dallas, and he joined Agudas Achim, an Orthodox congregation that was organized about 1925. He regularly walked to the congregation's Sabbath services. Originally started without a building, this small congregation held services in a feed store, and members sat on bales of hay or feed sacks. The congregation eventually purchased a small house on the corner of Forest Avenue and Wendelkin Street; however, the congregation was unable to survive when, a few decades later, most Jews moved out of this area of Dallas. Although Ben continued to practice more traditional forms of worship, Jenny rebelled at the Orthodox obligations. She did not like having to sit in the women's section of the congregation, and wishing to be thoroughly modern and American, she joined the Reform congregation, Emanu-El. She and the children attended Reform services, and the children attended the Emanu-El Sunday School.[10]

Although in past decades the lines between Reform, Conservative, and Modern Orthodox Jewish congregations have begun to blur, this was not the situation in 1930. Today some Reform congregations have restored various traditional practices, such as using more Hebrew in the service or wearing yarmulkes. Furthermore, both Reform and Conservative congregations might have a woman serve as rabbi or count women in their minyan.[11] However, the difference between the Reform congregations and the Orthodox congregations in Dallas during the early twentieth century would have been quite noticeable. Classical Reform services would have had mixed seating, and the primary service would have been held on Friday evening. Music and musical instruments would have been a part of the Reform services. Most of the service would have been conducted in English, with some Hebrew prayers scattered throughout the ceremony, and many of the congregants would not have kept kosher homes. The lives of the worshipers would also have differed. Orthodox families would have observed the dietary laws and refrained from eating pork, shellfish, and other forbidden foods, and the meat they ate would have been ritually slaughtered. They would not have mixed milk and meat, and many would not have driven, ridden, or worked on Saturday. They would have walked to religious services, and the Orthodox services would have been conducted primarily in Hebrew. Women sat in a walled-off section of the building, and the services would have started early on Saturday morning and continued until perhaps 1 p.m. More than likely, Ben was fluent in Hebrew and could fully take part in the services, whereas Jenny probably never learned Hebrew and felt more comfortable in the Reform congregation.

After arriving in Dallas, Ben expanded his real estate business and advertised that he was in the "banking and real estate business." Although he may have been selling some real estate, he also advertised that he made "loans." In fact, his advertisements offered cash for any kind of collateral a person had—automobiles, jewelry, homes, or businesses. It is not clear whether his children thought of their father as a banker, or a pawnbroker, or something else because he never advertised in the newspaper as a pawnbroker. Nevertheless, the current members of the Frankfurt family do think of him that way. During these decades his name also began

to appear in the legal section of the paper when he sued customers for failure to pay or when someone sued him for breach of contract. But it is unclear whether Ben was a real estate broker who also made loans on personal property or whether he was a pawnbroker who also made loans on real estate. Either way, he was a genuine wheeler-dealer who became more successful as the years passed. He eventually moved his family to University Park in the 1930s, and sometime in the 1940s he bought a house on Arcady Street in Highland Park—one of the most exclusive sections of Dallas.[12]

Dallas Business History and Jews in the Fashion Industry

During the first quarter of the twentieth century, Dallas evolved into a dynamic metropolitan area. In the late nineteenth century the city had been considered a "drummer's paradise." At that time, it was the only city in Texas with two crossing rail lines, one going east-west and one going north-south. Thus, salesmen could travel in all directions across the Southwest selling their goods. Additionally, the city council passed tax laws favorable to businesses, even making manufacturing plants tax exempt.[13] By the turn of the century, Dallas was developing into an economic hub, and the city government favored entrepreneurs. It was into this very energetic environment that Ben Frankfurt settled, and he could not have found a better place to live and raise a family of entrepreneurs.

During the nineteenth century Texas had welcomed immigrants, including Jews, and Jewish entrepreneurs had opened businesses in small and large towns across Texas. Moreover, new Jewish immigrants—primarily German Jews—usually arrived with some merchandising experience so that opening stores or shops became the natural means of earning a living.[14] During the nineteenth century many of the businessmen in the larger towns grew to become service merchants, wholesalers, and importers, but by the beginning of the twentieth century, this pattern of merchant growth had begun to change. In the twentieth century Jewish merchants in larger inland towns often evolved not into importers as merchants in coastal towns did but into jobbers and then manufacturers. Originally, all the higher-quality apparel items were brought into Texas from Europe or the East Coast, rather than being produced in Texas. Everyday and work clothes were locally manufactured at home or in small factories primarily for local distribution or to be sold to regional merchants.

Late in the nineteenth century Sanger Brothers of Dallas became one of the preeminent merchandising houses in the state, and it functioned as both a retailer and a wholesaler that distributed merchandise throughout Texas.[15] Most goods were imported into Texas, which did not actually manufacture the goods that were sold within its borders. By 1930 Jewish businessmen operated as jobbers for clothing manufacturers and as manufacturers in San Antonio, El Paso, Houston, Fort Worth, and Dallas, which became the hub for apparel manufacturing in the Southwest.[16] The prosperity of the Jewish merchants throughout Texas contributed to the prosperity of the area, and Dallas became a pleasant place to live.

Unlike cities in the North or Midwest, Dallas did not have an industrial base and no coal burning factories. It had begun as an agricultural and distributional center. Thus, it was a clean city that provided lighting from the nearby gas fields in East Texas, and according to Stanley Marcus, "it ha[d] a Southern Climate, Northern enterprise, Eastern sophistication and Western self-confidence."[17]

In 1914 based on Dallas's prosperity and the growth of businesses in the South, Dallas was selected as the site for one of the newly organized Federal Reserve banks. Ford Motor Company also opened a Dallas assembly plant at about the same time. These institutions contributed to the stability of the economy and brought more economic diversity to the city on the north Texas prairie. About ten years later Dallas had grown to become the forty-second largest city in the nation, with a growing workforce that included many young women. Dallas even boasted that 15,000 women from the area had joined the National Association of Business and Professional Women.

By the end of the 1930s, the Depression forced some Dallasites onto the relief roles. However, the discovery of oil in East Texas softened the spreading economic hardship and even put money into some residents' pockets. And Dallas was evolving from a center of regional commerce and a location from which drummers traveled throughout the state into a major hub for the garment industry. This economic diversity brought prosperity to Dallas and to the

Dallas Jewish population, and the Dallas Jewish community grew and thrived, especially with the contributions of larger Jewish merchants, jobbers, and garment manufacturers. [18]

Some of the Jewish merchants and manufacturers, such as the Sanger family, had arrived with the early wave of German immigrants who came to Texas during the mid-nineteenth century, but many of the men who settled in Dallas after the turn of the century arrived later with the wave of Eastern European immigrants. August Lorch emigrated from Germany around 1890 and was included in the Texas census of 1900. In that census he was listed as a dry-goods merchant, but by 1910 he had given up merchandising and had opened one of the first jobbing houses for ladies' wear in Dallas. Lorch represented several New York manufacturers who promised Lorch that all the lines they gave him were his alone—allowing him to claim that he carried "exclusive" styles. Soon, however, he discovered that another Dallas jobber was selling the same style line. This business conflict led to the beginning of the Lorch line of clothing, and by 1919 the unhappy Lorch was manufacturing ladies' clothing in Dallas. The Lorch Company became a pioneer manufacturing firm in Dallas.

The company began by manufacturing a line of cotton "house dresses" or low-end garments that sold for between $1.00 and $2.98. Around 1928 August Lorch decided he wanted to break into the better-dress market, and he brought Samuel Lambert to Dallas to oversee the production of silk dresses. This step propelled the Lorch Company into the upscale market and increased the firm's ability to compete with New York manufacturers of better dresses.

Lorch was not the only Jewish merchant who began as a jobber and shifted to manufacturing. Other Jewish businessmen from smaller towns in Texas, and even a few from as far away as New York, recognized that there were advantages to manufacturing in Dallas. Most importantly, at a time when unions were gaining strength in New York and the northeast, Dallas offered a nonunion workforce. Thus, garments manufactured in Dallas sold for less than similar garments manufactured in New York. Additionally, Dallas was more centrally located than were manufacturers on both coasts, and the proximity to southern and western markets reduced shipping expenses. Jewish firms in Dallas, such as Nardis, owned by Irving and Ben Gold, and Marcy Lee, owned by Lester Lief, Louis Marmar, and Earnest Wadel, along with Lorch, could sell to the small businesses throughout the Southwest and also compete favorably with East Coast manufacturers.[19] Jews in Dallas also owned and operated other clothing and accessories manufacturing plants; they were, for example, especially prominent in the millinery business. It was into this vibrant and vigorous world of fashion design and manufacturing that Edna Frankfurt Ravkind, Elsie Frankfurt, and eventually Louise Frankfurt Gartner eagerly marched forth and without hesitation entered what in Dallas was primarily a man's world.

Women in the Fashion World

Edna, Elsie, and Louise were unusual but not unique women in the fashion and business world. During the industrial revolution cloth and clothing manufacturing slowly moved from the home into shops and later into manufacturing plants. Manufactured cloth lowered the price of cloth and eventually reduced the relative cost of clothing. The invention of the sewing machine and subsequent garment factories lowered the prices of many clothing items even further. Men's garments, especially work clothes, were the first to be mass produced, while ladies' garments, especially those for middle-class and upper-class women, were the last to succumb to mass production. Most women's clothing items were created by women, a fact that provided an opportunity for women to become entrepreneurs. Besides clothing design and production the only other opportunity that women had to become entrepreneurs was in the beauty industry, a business that developed after the turn of the twentieth century, when beauty aids and cosmetics became acceptable for respectable women.

Women had entered the general workplace early in the nineteenth century, when they filled positions in cloth mills or did piecework at home or in shops. These women were young and single. They were able to leave the farm and the homestead because the industrial revolution made life on the farm easier and their labor was no longer needed at home. Other than millwork few opportunities were open to women. One of the few positions a woman could find, and perhaps the only position where a woman might become her own boss, was dressmaking. At a time when even teaching was mostly a man's job, dressmaking was one of the few professions available to women.

Cynthia Amnéus, author of *A Separate Sphere: Dressmakers in Cincinnati's Golden Age, 1877–1922*, has explained that, although dressmaking placed women in the commercial world, women still remained separated from men because in the nineteenth century men rarely designed women's clothes. Moreover, even in smaller cities or communities a seamstress or dressmaker could find patrons since even middle-class women often purchased the dresses they wore out in public.[20] Even middle-class women wanted one or two high-fashion garments made from silk or fine wool, and despite the cost of made-to-measure garments, shopgirls and other working women occasionally ordered dresses from seamstresses. These young working women often splurged on themselves and bought a Sunday dress from a seamstress. Finally, women often purchased custom-made garments when they wanted a wedding gown or needed mourning garments quickly.[21]

Dressmaking as a business attracted both single women and married or widowed women alike. For some single women becoming a dressmaker allowed them to maintain their own life and not be dependent on any man. Furthermore, dressmakers could open a dressmaking establishment with less capital than it took to open a mercantile shop. Widows sometimes had an advantage because they might have some extra funds after the death of their husbands and could purchase additional stocks or finer fabrics. If they were successful, they could even hire extra seamstress to work in their shop. Good seamstresses found customers from referrals and rarely needed to rely on paid advertisements.

Amnéus documented many Cincinnati, Ohio, dressmakers in her work *A Separate Sphere*. But perhaps the most thoroughly documented twentieth-century story of one dressmaker's shop was preserved at the Rhode Island School of Design Museum. This exhibit presents the story of the Tirocchi sisters of Providence, Rhode Island. Anna and Laura Tirocchi were examples of women entrepreneurs who arrived in America as immigrants and created a middle-class life for themselves by becoming high-fashion, couture dressmakers. Anna Tirocchi and Laura Tirocchi Cella were trained in Rome and immigrated to the United States about 1905. They opened their own business in 1911 and offered European styles created from imported fabrics. Because of their training and the fact that they spoke English, they could attract the most affluent Providence women. Their business grew, and eventually they employed about a dozen other women. For several decades they thrived, but the business struggled during the Depression, and the sisters eventually phased out custom-made garments.[22] The story of these sisters provides an example of how women could become business successes on their own and how the changing world of high fashion eventually forced them to alter their vision of their business operations.

Demand for custom-made garments remained strong through the end of the nineteenth century and into the first decades of the twentieth century. Although manufactured garments were customary in menswear by 1900, only about 10 percent of women's clothing was ready-made. In fact, many department stores carried piece goods and employed seamstresses to create customers' dresses copied from the latest New York or European styles. This practice continued throughout the early decades of the twentieth century.[23] By 1930 most women had given up ordering from dressmakers and had begun to shop in department stores. This change was spurred on by the democratization of fashion and easy access to well-made clothing. Instead of waiting weeks for a garment, a woman could shop in a department store, have the dress altered to fit, and have it hanging in her closet before the week was out.

During the decades when women's clothing evolved from custom-made to ready-to-wear, Dallas boasted one of the first fine department stores to offer only fashionable women's ready-to-wear. Neiman Marcus opened in 1907. Carrie Marcus Neiman, one of the owners of Neiman Marcus, was one of the first entrepreneurs to limit her merchandise to high-fashion, ready-made garments.

Besides dressmaking, the only other area in which women entrepreneurs flourished was the cosmetic or beauty industry—another field where men rarely competed. In 1900 the beauty trade was small and scattered around the country. Often local practitioners or pharmacists sold beauty products as a sideline business. But as society norms changed and wearing cosmetics became acceptable, the "beauty business" boomed, becoming the tenth-largest industry in the United States. This business was also owned and run primarily by women.

Originally seen as a trade or craft, not a business or profession, this industry was open to women, both black and white. Two of the first women to become wealthy in the beauty business were Annie Turnbo Malone and Madam C. J. Walker, black women entrepreneurs. Both these businesswomen got their start between the late 1890s and early 1900s. Both women traveled around the country, promoting their products and speaking to gatherings of black women, encouraging self-improvement, economic achievement, and self-respect. Malone and Walker began with specialty products manufactured for hair care for black women. They both hired and trained their own saleswomen to represent the products to other women, and they educated women to become economically independent and politically knowledgeable. These women became millionaires, as did other women who entered the cosmetic business early in the twentieth century, women such as Elizabeth Arden and Helena Rubenstein. Mary Kay Ash, a later entrant into the cosmetic business, modeled her business along the same lines as Walker and promoted the economic mobility of her sales associates. Most of these businesses, like many businesses owned by women, were originally funded from within—without bank financing, as Page Boy did.[24]

During the first half of the twentieth century, most women became business leaders only after they had opened their own businesses. However, one woman overcame all obstacles to become the president of one of the leading department stores based in New York. Dorothy Shaver, born in Arkansas and educated at the University of Arkansas and the University of Chicago, became the first woman president of a major firm. In 1921 Shaver moved to New York, and in 1924 she was hired by Lord & Taylor to head their department of comparative shopping. Twenty-two years later Shaver was named president of the company—the first woman to hold such a position at a major firm.[25]

Many of these successful women gave up part of their lives to become business entrepreneurs. Walker died at the age of fifty-one after suffering medical problems; Malone went through two divorces; and Shaver never married. Elizabeth Arden divorced both of her husbands, and Rubenstein also had a tumultuous private life. Even two of Texas's own remarkable women entrepreneurs endured unhappy marriages. Carrie Marcus Neiman divorced her unfaithful husband and never remarried, and Enid Justin, daughter of Joseph Justin (who started Justin Boots), herself the owner of Nacona Boot Company, which became one of the top five bootmakers in the United States, experienced a similar life event. Such trials in their personal lives demonstrate that running a business during the early 1900s put strains on women's personal lives. Even the Frankfurt sisters had unusual personal lives. Edna became the breadwinner, and her husband Abe became the primary-care provider for their children. Elsie married after the business became successful, and although she never admitted her age, she was past fifty when she married. Only Louise, who left Page Boy after about twenty years, lived what would be considered at the time a conventional married life.

Writing the Story of Page Boy

This story is not just the story of three sisters. It is also the story of the business they created. Bringing their story to life has been a significant undertaking; however, it has been filled with excitement and difficulties. One of the most difficult problems to overcome when telling the full story of Page Boy, and especially when assessing the successes and failures of the firm, was the total lack of a business archive: financial documents, partnership records, and corporate minutes. Private corporations are not required to file financial documents with the government or any regulatory agency, but they should have these documents in their business files. Additionally, there were no employment records to indicate the number or classification of Page Boy employees; thus it was impossible to ascertain the capacity in which Page Boy actually hired and paid nonfamily employees. A thorough search in archival sources produced only one set of financial documents, and even though I had access to family members, I was never able to uncover any business documents. Gigi Gartner arranged for me to interview her mother, Louise Frankfurt Gartner, and I have spoken and corresponded with Louise's other daughter, Brenda Berg. Neither of these women was involved in the business and so knew very little about the actual business of Page Boy. Penny Pollock has granted me complete access to the Page Boy scrapbooks and other papers and documents that were kept by her stepmother, Elsie Frankfurt Pollock, and she shared her experiences of working for Page Boy during its last years. I located one copy of ownership records, balance sheet, and income statement dated 1963 in the Steve Carlin Papers, housed at the University of Texas Center for American History. These documents offer a snapshot of that year but only indicate the owners' names and some semblance of an income statement from the early 1960s; they did not reflect total assets. These scant papers provided no information about the first two decades or the final three decades of Page Boy's business and financial history.

Finally, there is no information about the relationships between and among the sisters. Edna died in 2002, and Elsie was unavailable for an interview; she died in January 2011. Although Louise consented to be interviewed, she gave no explanation of her departure from the firm other than that she wanted to spend more time at home. Finally, there was no explanation for the discontinuation of wholesaling, a radical step, other than what Edna had said in one interview: her comment indicated that she could not manage the operations in Dallas and oversee the wholesale distribution of Page Boy merchandise.

And Elsie simply declared she did not want to deal with returns. But there was no mention of hiring or promoting someone to take over some of these responsibilities, and it is possible that this decision led to the eventual demise of the firm. No documentation explained the financial strength or weakness of the company or whether Edna and Elsie ever considered going public—although Elsie's stepdaughter, Penny Pollock, argues that Page Boy was Elsie's baby and that she would not have wanted to give custody of her child to others. Going public might not have saved Page Boy, but other firms, such as Elizabeth Arden, Estée Lauder, and Liz Claiborne evolved into public companies and still exist. But one might ask whether, if Page Boy had lived on into the future, it would have been the same company. The Frankfurt sisters created a firm that specialized in well-made, upscale clothes, and it is questionable whether this model could have been continued on a large scale and without these women.

Despite the dearth of business data, I was able to glean a wealth of information from eight large Page Boy scrapbooks. The scrapbooks were custom-made, with the Page Boy logo imprinted on the front cover. These books were maintained by Elsie Frankfurt Pollock and were loaned to the author by Penny Pollock. The scrapbooks contained newspaper clippings from all over the United States and even some from foreign countries. They also contained many short stories that appeared in magazines along with magazine advertisements. Some books were specialized and contained only magazine and other periodical clippings, while others contained mixed documents. The earliest articles were from the late 1940s. Other scrapbooks contained items such as the Page Boy nine-month calendar, which was provided to customers in the 1950s, and pages from one of Page Boy's brochures. With the scrapbooks came a box of Page Boy catalogs that dated from the 1950s through the sale of the business. Some of these brochures were dated and others were not. The family also graciously shared private photographs with me.

Chapter 1

From a Dilemma to a Delightful Solution: Making Maternity Skirts Fit

Popular belief suggests that in previous centuries women secluded themselves during pregnancy. However, a closer examination of the lives of women and their clothing indicates that this was not always the case.[1] As early as the fourteenth century, artists depicted the pregnant Madonna and other women wearing the clothing of the era. Although these dresses were not maternity clothes, they were garments altered for a pregnant body. Giotto, one of the finest artists of the late Middle Ages, who introduced a new style of art that accurately represented scenes, included pregnant women in his art. His women wore garments gathered under the bust that were divided on the sides, showing their undergarments. Two centuries later, when women wore short bodices with flowing skirts, they looked pregnant whether they were or not.[2] Even a review of artwork created from the beginning of the 1700s through the early nineteenth century indicates that pregnant women were often included in group scenes depicting urban settings. Perhaps only with the advent of the Victorian era did women become reclusive while pregnant. Moreover, the belief that women secluded themselves during pregnancy would only be true of the more affluent women, since women who were less affluent would need to work—pregnant or not.

During the seventeenth and eighteenth centuries many middle-class women supervised their homes or managed, along with their husbands, small commercial establishments. These women were unable to remain secluded multiple times during their numerous pregnancies. In some instances they trekked around town doing the business of the household, and they continued to entertain while pregnant. For example, the nature of life in villages or towns required women to go to the market or to deal with customers if the husband was away. Moreover, when one considers that many of these women were often pregnant for half the time between marriage and middle age, it is understandable that they continued their daily activities throughout their pregnancies. Even those women of higher status who could have remained secluded because they had servants to make necessary purchases did not forgo daily activities. Because these women continued to participate in regular daily life, they needed clothing that was altered or made especially for maternity wear.[3]

Even though women needed clothing to cover the pregnant body,[4] often the clothes were not necessarily created solely for maternity use. During the seventeenth, eighteenth, and early nineteenth century textiles were quite expensive, and garments were often altered from year to year, season to season, or for use by the pregnant woman and then back for the nonpregnant woman. Linda Baumgarten's study of late eighteenth-century women's clothing indicates that many garments were either created with extra material or panels so that the garments could be let out, or else they were made in a way so that one part of the garment could be enlarged or changed for various uses. For example, a peplum could be widened or created with pleats to cover the increasing size of the abdomen. Often side seams were cut with extra fabric so that the garment could be made larger to accommodate the increased girth of the pregnant woman. Some women solved the

problem of the expanding body by wearing "bed-gowns" under a larger waistcoat or apron. The bedgown was a loosely fitted dress that could serve as a nightgown or undergarment but was also used as part of the maternity wardrobe. In some instances women, especially those who worked in a shop, used these loosely fitted garments along with an over-garment similar to a jumper or apron. Other women solved the problem by wearing "waistcoats" or vests that were laced in both the back and front. The laces could be let out or taken up to accommodate either the pregnant or the nonpregnant body. Additionally, some garments had extra fabric under the armholes so that a pregnant woman or nursing mother could accommodate larger breasts.[5]

With the advent of the power loom and later the sewing machine, textiles and then ready-made clothing were less expensive and more readily available, and even custom-made dresses were less expensive than they had previously been. Middle-class women could afford dresses that changed when the fashions changed, and they could afford dresses created for various specific uses. Thus, they could also make or purchase dresses that were comfortable during the times that they were pregnant. Nevertheless, the dilemma of the expanding body and how to cover it remained a constant problem.

While Linda Baumgarten argues that women during the eighteenth century continued their activities and participated in both social and commercial events during their pregnancy, Rebecca Bailey suggests that, due to medical advice and changing cul-

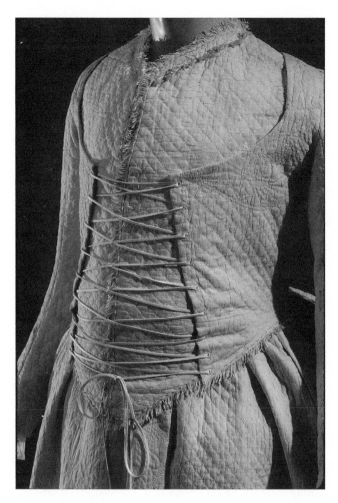

Lace-up vest from Colonial Williamsburg, early eighteenth century. Reprinted by permission of the Colonial Williamsburg Foundation. Museum Purchase.

tural norms, pregnant middle-class women in the second half of the nineteenth century often decreased their activities and lived secluded lives. But these women still needed maternity clothing for use at home, and several specific design problems remained unsolved. The first problem was how one comfortably allows for the expanding abdomen, and second was how one keeps the dress or skirt from appearing shorter in the front when it hikes up as it covers the growing abdomen. These problems are the same whether one is creating a one-piece dress hanging from the shoulders or a two-piece outfit with the skirt hanging over the abdomen.

These problems were exacerbated after the turn of the twentieth century as fashion and women's lives began to change. Whereas during most of the nineteenth century women wore fashions that were created with many layers of fabric and also used excessive yardage in the designs, in the twentieth century fashion designs began to hug the female form. Women also began to discard the multiple layers of undergarments that had been popular in earlier decades. Also, as the Victorian era waned, time-saving devices and the advent of electric appliances made housekeeping less time consuming, and more women became involved in various activities outside the home. Some even began to work out of the house, and each of these activities increased the need for more garments. In addition, the expansion of the middle class created an increasing demand for ready-made clothing.[6] However, ready-made maternity dresses were difficult to find.

In 1904 Lena Bryant became perhaps the first designer and manufacturer to market maternity clothing. Bryant borrowed funds from her family to establish her business, and when she went to the bank to open an account with these funds, the bank misspelled her name. The misspelling stuck, and her business became Lane Bryant. Bryant made individual dresses and hung them up for sale, displaying them as if they were ready-made outfits. Her first experience in designing maternity clothing came when she received a request to make a maternity dress that was "practical for entertaining at home."[7] This request encouraged seamstress Bryant to include maternity dresses in her line of ready-made garments. Rebecca Bailey suggests that eventually Lena Bryant dropped her maternity line as her business grew and she became the first clothing manufacturer specializing in clothing for the fuller-figured woman, now known as Lane Bryant.[8] However, a close examination of newspaper advertisements that appeared between 1920 and 1950 indicates that Lane Bryant continued to manufacture maternity garments into the 1950s. These garments, though, were not created for the upscale market. For example, in 1937 Lane Bryant advertised three maternity dresses that ranged in price from $3.95 to $6.95.[9] The advertising copy stated that all three dresses did their "clever bit to reapportion the figure, all have concealed adjustable features." But all were dresses that either wrapped around the body or hung from the shoulders.[10] Thus, although Lane Bryant was manufacturing maternity dresses, the company had not solved the problem of the expanding abdomen and the uneven hemline.

The problem of how to cover the pregnant abdomen became more pronounced as the twentieth century progressed and skirts got shorter. Perhaps one of the first inventors to try to solve these problems was Robert Peters. In 1907 he applied for and was granted a patent for a skirt that he claimed would solve the problem of maternity skirts. His skirt "contained no drawstrings or lacings," but it could be adjusted to fit the expanding waist of the wearer. The Peters skirt pattern had a fabric-covered waistband made of spring steel that was divided into two parts. The parts wrapped around the waist and overlapped on the sides. The two pieces were held in place by a system of multiple metal hooks and eyes. As the waist enlarged the woman could move the hooks so that they could loosen the garment. Peters's invention also offered a way for the band to rise above the actual waist because the front section of the metal band could swivel up, arching over the abdomen. This band could be enlarged, but it remained rigid around the body, like a metal belt. To compensate for the change in skirt length as the front section of the band was raised above the abdomen, an oval panel with a flap extension of fabric was attached to the top front of the skirt.[11] Although in theory Peters's patent solved the problem, his design did not become the standard in maternity wear. First, not many women would have wanted a steel band hooked around their waists, especially when they were pregnant; moreover, there is no proof that Peters ever converted his

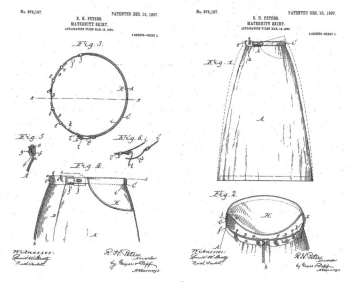

Patent 873,167 of 1907

idea into an actual salable garment or that he profited from his invention.[12]

Two years after Peters's invention was patented, W. Padernacht obtained a patent for another adjustable skirt. This skirt had two parallel vertical slits and a band that could be adjusted with hooks folded into grommets. Each V-shaped slit could be widened as the abdomen enlarged. But this skirt patent did not include an upper garment so there was no corresponding plan to conceal the openings created by the slits.[13] Various designers or inventors continued to apply for and be granted patents for maternity clothing throughout the next few decades. A dress patent was granted in 1916 that included a wraparound empire-line garment with an expandable waist. But this garment, like the others, did not solve the problem of the hiking hemline.[14] Two more skirt

patents were issued in 1919, and during the mid-1930s the U.S. patent office issued two more patents for maternity dresses. Yet, because each of these garments hung from the shoulders with various forms of adjustments around the waist, neither solved the problem of the skirt hiking up over the abdomen, which caused the front section of the skirt to look shorter than the back.[15]

The manufacture and sale of all ready-made clothing slowed when the Depression hit, leaving unsolved the problem of how to cover the pregnant woman's body. Additionally, the Depression lowered the birthrate, decreasing the demand for maternity clothing. For women who were pregnant during the Depression, "a single style was made to serve" multiple situations.[16] During the 1930s, when women did shop for garments to wear when they were pregnant, they usually purchased dresses in larger and larger sizes, or they opted to wear a Hooverette, a wrap dress with two panels crossing in the front. These panels were cut so that they would cover the front but could expand across the enlarging abdomen. Neither of these options was satisfactory since the larger dresses had larger arm openings, sleeves, and shoulders, and bigger sizes were also generally longer from shoulder to waist and from waist to skirt bottom; thus they created a dowdy and unkempt appearance. The Hooverette had no waist and hung vertically from the shoulders with a tie attached at the waist, crossing around and tying on the side. But as the woman loosened the ties to accommodate the growing baby, there was no way for the garment to

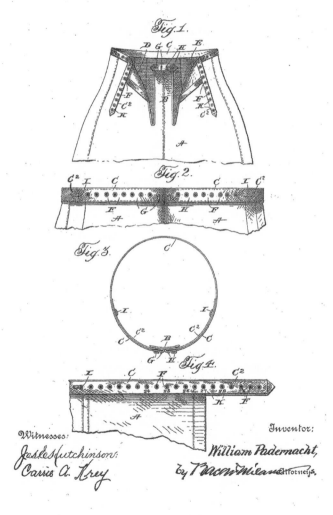

W. PADERNACHT.
MATERNITY SKIRT.
APPLICATION FILED AUG. 16, 1909.

960,689.

Patented June 7, 1910.

Fig.1.

Fig.2.

Fig.3.

Fig.4.

Witnesses:
Jas. Les Hutchinson.
Carrie A. Frey

Inventor:
William Padernacht,
by Bacon Milan Attorneys.

Patent 960,687 of 1910

lengthen to account for the increased length needed to cover the abdomen. As with previous attempts to solve the problem, the skirt front hiked up, becoming shorter in the front than around the sides and back.

This dilemma set the stage for the birth of Page Boy Maternity Company. In the 1930s Edna Frankfurt, Ben and Jenny Frankfurt's oldest daughter, worked as a secretary for Magnolia Petroleum Company in Dallas. In 1933 she married Abe Ravkind, but she continued to work.[17] In 1937, when she was pregnant with her second child, her sister Elsie noted that instead of looking well groomed and stylish as she usually did, Edna looked rumpled and frumpy. In fact, Elsie exclaimed, her sister looked like a "beach ball in an unmade bed." This situation inspired Elsie to create a new and novel design and later an innovative business plan for both herself and Edna and eventually the younger sister, Louise Frankfurt.[18]

Elsie, who had earned a double degree in accounting and design from Southern Methodist University, asserted that she could solve the problem of the expanding front by combining the skills she had gained in her engineering drawing class with her dress design training.[19] She pondered the problem that pregnant women had in covering the abdomen without hiking the skirt. Because Elsie concluded that pregnant women had shapes that were like babies—with no waistline—she believed that maternity garments must fit at the shoulders, have a top that covered the waistline, and then have a well-fitted skirt. Generating a design using engineering principles, she solved the dilemma by practicing on one of Edna's old prepregnancy suits. Elsie cut out a window in the front of the skirt and then worked out a system of loops and drawstrings to hold the skirt in place. With the hole cut in the front, she could fit the skirt snuggly around the hips and simultaneously maintain a level hemline by using the loops and tapes. Three days later Edna was wearing Elsie's new design, a navy, two-piece ensemble with an inverted pleat in the jacket back and front, and a white bow attached under a small collar. Elsie's design possessed all the flair of the well-fitted suits of the day. It had a slim skirt with a scooped opening in the front allowing the abdomen to expand through the window. The skirt was held up by several loops, and a fabric tape connected to each side of the waistband. The horizontal tape looped through the vertical tape and together they held the base of the skirt opening level. Her complete design also had a jacket that hung neatly from the shoulders and extended long enough to cover the hole in the skirt.[20]

According to most written accounts, Elsie, who had been musing about her future, had not been able to decide whether to look for a job in accounting or in design. But this novel design idea convinced her that she had solved her career problems—she would go into business manufacturing maternity suits. These two sisters were no Texas twits. They feared having their idea stolen so, according to most written accounts, Elsie marched herself right off to an attorney's offices to have the idea patented. The

Aug. 18, 1936.

A. E. HAISTER
MATERNITY DRESS
Filed Oct. 30, 1935

2,051,444

2 Sheets—Sheet 1

Fig. 1.

Fig. 2.

Inventor
Aaron E. Haister

By Clarence A. O'Brien, and Hyman Berman, Attorneys

Patent 2,051,444 of 1935

attorney evaluated her design and told her the idea could be patented but that it would cost three hundred dollars.[21]

It is worth noting that the exact story of how Elsie developed the pattern in her mind, and how she created the working model of the garment, and later how quickly the business came into being varied from publication to publication. The first accounts of the origin of the company did not appear in print until the firm was about ten years old, but within a few years multiple additional stories appeared in print. In one story, Elsie and her mother were sitting on their front porch when Edna, pregnant with her second child, walked up the steps. According to this story, Elsie made the frequently repeated statement, "You look like a beach ball in an unmade bed." At this point Edna explained that she was wearing her mother's dress because it was the only thing she could get on. In this story, published in 1950 by *Colliers*, it took Elsie three days to create the original design by cutting up one of Edna's prepregnancy suits. Additionally, according to this version of the narrative, when the sisters decided to start a business they combined their savings and scraped up a total of $501.22. They figured it would cost about that much to rent a shop, hire seamstresses, purchase fabric, and outfit the business. Yet, in another story published in 1949, the sisters borrowed the funds needed to start the business from their mother. In still another story about the beginning of Page Boy, Elsie Frankfurt said that when she commented about her pregnant sister's looks, Edna snapped, "I suppose you could do better" and that Elsie borrowed fabric from her mother, sat down at the family sewing machine, and designed the outfit with a slim skirt and a smart top.

In most versions of the beginning of the business, the sisters kept their business plans a secret from their father; however, in at least one version of the birth of the business, Elsie said that she and Edna approached their father, asking for a loan to start the business. According to that story, their father "was quite open-handed with business advice, but . . . the other hand remained in his pocket," leaving the girls to scrape up the funds themselves. In still another account, one of the few that quotes Louise Frankfurt Gartner, Louise indicated that when the older sisters were searching for funds, she had twenty-five dollars in her savings account, which she contributed to her sisters so they could start the business.[22]

In any case, the sisters obtained the funds to begin the business, and during the summer of 1937, Edna and Elsie continued to make plans to open their shop. They debated about how to set up the business, where to open the shop, and what to call the business. Elsie claimed she called her sister one hot August night, exclaiming that she had had an epiphany and that they should call the new firm "Page Boy" after the small boy blowing a trumpet who announced the birth of an heir to the throne. Elsie added that she thought they could also trademark the picture of a small boy blowing a trumpet. Edna agreed and added that she knew exactly where the shop should be—the Medical Arts Building. The next day the sisters rented a ground-floor shop in that building and began making arrangements to remodel the space.

During the next few months Edna served as a walking advertisement for Elsie's design, and she quickly began getting inquiries from friends who wanted copies of the suit. At this point the sisters knew they had a winner. Before the store opened Edna and Elsie rented a loft to use as a workshop, hired two seamstresses, and began selling outfits to friends. Shortly before they opened for business, they had plush carpet installed in the small shop and added soft pastel paint to the walls. Finally they installed muted lighting to improve the ambiance of the shop. Mrs. Jenny Frankfurt, their mother, worked in the shop helping Edna and Elsie organize the displays and hang curtains. Some stories say that one day, when everyone was busily working on the displays, Mrs. Frankfurt commented that she hoped that Mr. Frankfurt did not find out about their plans before the shop opened. According to these stories, Ben Frankfurt suddenly appeared in the shop entrance. Startled, Mrs. Frankfurt asked him how he had found them. He replied that he was seeing his doctor in the building, and the doctor had just asked what he thought about "his girls" opening a maternity dress shop in the building. Ben Frankfurt was never impressed with his daughters' business ideas.[23] Nevertheless, he decided to wait and see whether their venture succeeded or not.

Many of the written accounts say that the shop opened in either 1938 or even as late as 1939. However, a small advertisement appeared in the *Dallas Morning News* on December 5, 1937, announcing the opening of the Page Boy Maternity Shop on the ground floor of the Medical Arts Building on St. Paul Street,[24] proving that the shop actually opened earlier than most written accounts indicate. This discrepancy in the actual opening date does not detract from the fact that Edna's idea of opening the business in the Medical Arts Building proved to be a strategic success. Since many obstetricians had their offices in that building, most pregnant women passed by the Page Boy window on their way to their appointments. Again, the story has multiple versions and gets twisted in retelling.

That the patent was not filed until six months after the shop opened—despite the story about Elsie's running out to find a lawyer—indicates that she did not file for the patent as soon as the design was created. The patent request was filed on June 3, 1938, and six months later, on December 27, 1938, about a year after the shop opened, the United States government granted E. Frankfurt et al. patent number 2,141,814 for a maternity garment ensemble.[25] The patent gave Edna Frankfurt Ravkind and Elsie Frankfurt sole rights to the innovative design. Although according to many stories Elsie and Edna applied for the patent almost as soon as Elsie worked the design out on paper and in fabric, it must have taken at least six months for Elsie and Edna to hire an attorney, get the design down on paper and the drawings accurately rendered, and apply for the patent. Moreover, by compressing the time between envisioning the skirt with a window, applying for a patent, and opening the shop, Elsie could make the account sound more spectacular, and by moving the shop opening to 1938 or 1939, it was easier for her to shave years from her age. Claiming to be younger than she actually was became a constant ploy that Elsie practiced throughout her life. At first, she only changed her age by a few years, but by 1963 when she provided some financial information to Dun & Bradstreet, she indicated that she had been born in 1918 instead of 1911 and that Edna had been born in 1914 instead of 1907. This allowed each sister to shave seven years from her age.

In 1938, several months before the patent had been submitted for approval, an article appeared in the Dallas paper describing Page Boy's new spring designs. This article is perhaps the first time that a fashion writer mentioned Page Boy's outfits in a comprehensive article about women's clothing; it indicates that the sisters were actually in production prior to filing the patent request. Elisabeth King Scott's article described the new spring lines of clothing being shown in Dallas—including Page Boy. Many of the new spring creations were designed using floral print fabrics with flower trimmings. Scott added, "Even the expectant mothers may have her floral-printed frock." She added that Page Boy outfits were also available in dark sheers with floral buttons. "The new 'Page Boy' maternity dresses are offered in many lovely fabrics and colors," and outfits were in fact available in silks, alpaca, linen, and

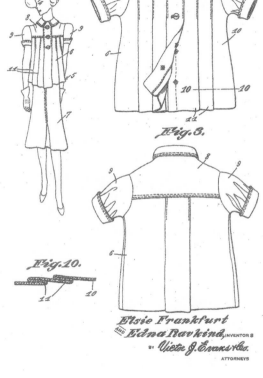

Patent 2,141,814, 1938

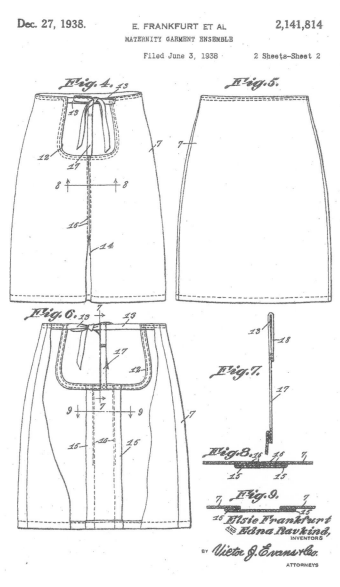

MATERNITY GARMENT ENSEMBLE

Filed June 3, 1938   2 Sheets—Sheet 2

Fig.4.

Fig.5.

Fig.6.

Fig.7.

Fig.8.

Fig.9.

Elsie Frankfurt
AND Edna Ravkind,
INVENTORS

BY Victor J. Evans & Co.
ATTORNEYS

Patent 2,141,814, 1938

chiffon. Scott continued, "The skirt is so fashioned that it fits correctly and smoothly. The blouse is designed with box pleats in the back and front so that it hangs loose but with a fashionable flare."[26]

The first Page Boy shop was only large enough to house a small showroom, one dressing room, and a tiny workroom in the rear. In the beginning two seamstresses made and altered the suits, and Edna and Elsie did the selling. The original designs sold for $22.95 retail and $12.50 wholesale. According to several of Elsie's interviews, Page Boy had netted $3,000 by the summer of 1938, only a few months after it opened.[27]

According to Elsie, as soon as they sold the dresses they had in stock, she rushed around Dallas searching through all the department stores that sold textiles and purchased fabric retail. Then she would hurry the fabric to the seamstresses so that they could cut and make more outfits. Elsie would assist the seamstresses in fashioning the dresses, and often she did alterations for customers herself. Elsie's marketing instincts helped the firm expand the sales territory. After one of her friends told her that she was planning a trip to Atlanta, Elsie asked her to wear one of the outfits and walk into J. P. Allen's, a department store. Without an appointment with the buyer or manager, the friend did as requested. As a result of that visit, Page Boy received a telegram, asking whether they would sell the dresses wholesale, and Page Boy sold thirty-six dresses to the Allen store.

After a few months of this hectic system, Elsie

realized that she needed to stop purchasing fabric retail, and she scheduled a visit to New York.[28] Elsie knew that she needed enough time to make the dresses and sell them before the invoice for the fabric became due, but one after another, the fabric manufacturers turned down her request for fabric to be shipped to the new firm on an "open account." Without a credit rating the fabric brokers and manufacturers turned the "little girl" down. In desperation, Elsie arrived at the sales office of Celanese Fabrics. Using all her Southern charm and persuasive talents, she convinced Celanese to ship the fabric and wait to be paid. Within a few weeks of receiving the fabric, Page Boy paid the account in full, and shortly after that Dun & Bradstreet offered the firm a rating.[29]

A few months later, another friend visited New York and stopped in at Best & Company while wearing a Page Boy design. She, too, left the store with another order. Undaunted, the friend later walked into Associated Merchandising Corporation, a supplier for various department stores from coast to coast and spoke to the buyer. As a result of this visit, Page Boy sold dresses to merchants from Seattle to New Orleans. After receiving these orders, Elsie realized that they needed a better space to manufacture the dresses, and she leased a space on Main Street for forty dollars a month.[30]

By the middle of 1939, Page Boy designs were being advertised across the country. The *Los Angeles Times* carried several advertisements for maternity outfits with the "adjustable skirt." The advertising

SUMMER "PAGE BOY" IN COOL CHAMBRAY

12.95

Best & Co. advertisement of an early
Page Boy design, 1939

copy indicated that the styles sold for between $12.95 and $22.95. The paper did not state where the dresses were being sold. Instead, it advised customers to call a local phone number or write to a California address.[31] In New York, Best & Company advertised, "Having a baby? Our 'Page Boy' is the ideal frock for you." The copy emphasized that the skirt was "not wrap-around." The outfit sold for $22.95 and came in black, green, wine, and peacock.[32] J. P. Allen & Co. in Atlanta advertised, "A new Collection of 'Page Boy' maternity dresses. The fame and popularity of our exclusive Page Boy have gained by leaps and bounds since first we introduced them to Atlanta mothers-to-be!" Allen carried models that ranged in price from $17.95 to $25.00 and offered dinner-length skirts for $14.95.[33] All these outfits utilized similar designs: a long jacket that hung long enough to cover the window in the skirt. By the end of the second year, Page Boy manufactured a full range of styles in a variety of colors, including suits in silk, alpaca, linen, chiffon, cotton, and in solid colors and prints.[34]

In March of 1939, Elsie took another step to promote sales: she wrote a column for the Dallas newspaper. She asserted that pregnant women often hid under large coats even during warm weather because they felt unstylish and frumpy. She emphasized that these women could look stylish, and she advised planning the maternity wardrobe with multipurpose pieces. Elsie even provided examples, suggesting that women could purchase two items suitable for church and going out and another for shopping or an "afternoon of bridge."[35] By the end of the decade, Page Boy had become a full-line manufacturer making clothing for all occasions. Furthermore, the shop had begun to sell maternity brassieres.

According to Rosalie Ravkind, who had been Edna's daughter-in-law, Edna recounted an incident that took place shortly after the shop started carrying brassieres. A customer came in to see dresses and then decided she wanted to try on the bras also. The woman could not find the correct size so she asked for help. Neither of the sisters had learned how to fit a bra and, because they were slender, neither had any experience fitting women with larger breasts. When the woman asked for advice and assistance, the sisters were stunned. They had no idea how to measure the woman so the only thing they could do was run back and forth from the fitting room to the stock of bras pulling one style after another and asking the customer what she thought. At the end of the session, both women were exhausted.[36]

Chapter 2

From a Pregnant Idea to the Post-War Boom

By the beginning of 1940, American commercial activity had begun to increase because America was supplying Europe with war goods. Some Americans were beginning to feel that the Depression was fading, and they felt better about their own financial situation. By this time Edna and Elsie had at least two years of experience in the business of manufacturing maternity clothing, and the company appeared to be a success. In about 1940 Edna and her family took a vacation to California and visited Los Angeles. While there, she saw what she believed was a perfect spot for a second Page Boy shop. Located at 3022 Wilshire Boulevard, it was in the hub of the upscale shopping area.[1] Edna called Elsie, declaring that she wanted to rent the space and open a shop in Los Angeles. Enthusiasm overtook the sisters, and while still on vacation Edna rented the location she had seen. While discussing this new shop, the sisters decided that they would not attempt to manage the business long distance. Instead, they decided that one of the sisters needed to relocate to the West Coast. So Edna, her husband, and two children, along with a nanny, moved to Venice Beach, California. Edna oversaw the opening and operation of the new store in California, and Elsie managed the main office, the manufacturing factory, and the retail store in Dallas.[2] After opening the Los Angeles shop, Page Boy regularly advertised in the *Los Angeles Times*.[3]

According to one story, on Edna's first day in the new California shop, she unlocked the door and heard the phone ringing. The voice on the other end of the line asked whether the store would be open until six that night. Edna answered in the affirmative. At 5:45 a woman arrived and bought a complete maternity wardrobe, including formal gowns, dresses, casual outfits, and beach wear. "I couldn't come earlier," she said. "I'm on location." Edna took the check and scrutinized the signature—it was that of Margaret Sullivan.[4]

Although Edna was living in California and managing the shop there, Elsie insisted on also being directly involved in the shop's daily operations. In an age when not many people flew back and forth across the country, Elsie regularly flew from Dallas to Los Angeles so that she could keep an eye on her sister and the California operation. In fact, her travels to California were often noted in the "To and From Dallas" column of the *Dallas Morning News.*[5]

About the same time that Edna and Elsie had started Page Boy, Louise, the youngest sister, entered the University of Illinois at Champaign. In 1941, after graduating with honors in dress design, Louise (called "Tootsie") returned to Dallas from Champaign. She was returning to Dallas only for the summer since she had won a scholarship to a design school in New York and planned to continue her studies there. Edna was still living in California, and she begged Louise to stay in Dallas. Edna argued that the firm needed a full-time designer and that there was too much work in Dallas for Elsie to manage alone. After weeks of being wheedled and cajoled, Louise gave in and decided to stay in Dallas, joining the firm as the primary designer,[6] thus creating a dynamic company where all three sisters focused on making pregnant women fashionable.

The sisters never wanted to lose an opportunity for a sale and sold the sample dresses that were produced while creating a design. They even sold designs that never made it into production. These sales of designs that were not successful brought in extra cash and profited Dallas women who had access to these one-of-a kind designs at discounted prices. One evening in 1942, Elsie and her date went to dinner with another Jewish couple. The young woman was pregnant and wearing one of the Page Boy samples. Elsie looked over the design, scrutinized the trim and finally said, "I should have changed those buttons and altered this trim."[7] Clearly, even after a design was in production, Elsie's mind was constantly considering how to improve a dress, even those already in production, demonstrating her business acumen and focus. The design process was never completed.

By 1942 the Page Boy logo—the small page boy holding a trumpet—and the name were recognized from coast to coast. The firm had outlets in Atlanta, New York, Cincinnati, Chicago, and California and its Dallas headquarters. Even Hollywood recognized the smartness of Page Boy designs. In 1942 Metro Goldwin Mayer announced that it would produce a short film entitled "What about Daddy?" The film, which starred Mary Shepherd, Dorothy Morris, and David O'Brien, told the story of a pregnant woman and her husband and featured maternity clothing manufactured by the Page Boy firm. In one scene Dorothy Morris wore a two-piece outfit with a solid color skirt and a top of narrow stripes. The blouse had short sleeves and a small bow that matched the skirt. In another scene she wore a two-piece dress with a mandarin collar. The skirt and top were made of the same fabric.[8]

At this time both Louise and Elsie were designing for Page Boy. Early in 1943 the company planned a multiple-piece mix-and-match maternity wardrobe. Although the outfits were not advertised under the Page Boy logo, Sylvia Weaver, in her column for the *Los Angeles Times*, described a six-piece wardrobe that cost $40.00. The wardrobe consisted of a three-piece cotton outfit—skirt, jacket, and slacks that were sold together and cost $10.95; a blouse for $2.98; a cotton dress for $6.95, and a wool jumper that cost less than $20.00. As with other articles she wrote, Weaver instructed her readers to call or write to the address she provided at the bottom of the article.

Between 1940 and 1942 Page Boy advertised in the *Los Angeles Times*. In June of 1941, the firm announced, "Elsie Frankfurt, Page Boy's foremost designer is here this week for consultation." The next year, 1942, Page Boy announced again, "We're expecting, Too! [The California store was expecting Elsie for a visit.] Elsie Frankfurt creator of the Page Boy Fashions arrives today and gladly will advise you on smart clothes."[9] At this time, Edna lived in Los Angeles and managed the store, but Louise had also moved to California, where she set up a small workshop in the rear of the Wilshire Boulevard store. It is obvious that even though both Edna and Louise were living in California, Elsie wanted to be part of the California activities and frequently flew to California.

She also remained Page Boy's voice in the press. When she arrived she used her own name in store promotions, not Edna's or Louise's name. Just before the war broke out, Louise began to learn the business side of the organization because Page Boy was planning to open a shop in San Francisco, and Louise was training to be the manager of the new shop. But the sisters never completed these plans.[10]

Just as Page Boy embarked on a plan of expansion, the United States entered World War II. The war impacted businesses but also forced many families to reconsider their family living circumstances. Many young families and especially single women returned home. With Edna and her family living in California and Louise ready to move to San Francisco alone, the sisters reconsidered their situation. Travel became difficult, preventing Elsie from easily commuting to the West Coast. Moreover, many families drew closer together, and Louise along with Edna and her family returned to Dallas.[11]

By this time the United States had begun preparing for war; however, much of the early preparations did not affect small businesses. The government's increasing industrial orders all went to larger firms, while smaller firms continued to supply non-military customers if materials allowed. Nevertheless, as the United States prepared for war, Congress began to worry about the stability of small businesses, which were called "small fellows" in the congressional hearings. But with increased production of war goods, some supplies became scarce, and continued mobilization intensified the problem of allocating scarce commodities. To help with this problem, in August of 1941, President Roosevelt created the Supply Priorities and Allocation Board (SPAB). With the help of this committee, some medium-size firms were guaranteed a share of the military orders, especially as subcontractors. After this change the SPAB focused on helping small firms supply essential civilian goods.[12] All these preparations had little effect on Page Boy's ability to supply its customers; however, the changes did have some effect on how the firm obtained fabric and other necessities for manufacturing.

Early in the preparations for war, clothing manufacturing had not been impacted by the mobilization. However, once the United States declared war on Japan, war regulations severely restricted the amount of fabric available to all civilian clothing manufacturers, thus creating restrictions on designers' freedom of expression. Small firms were squeezed in multiple ways. First, they were generally prevented from bidding on government contracts, so they could not convert their production to supplying military projects. Second, rationing of materials resulted in severe limits to their productivity for the civilian market. In fact, the government recognized this problem when on December 10, 1941, Donald Nelson, coordinator of national defense purchases for the War Production Board, commented that small manufacturers were "in serious trouble" because they could not obtain government contracts and regulations severely limited their production. Nelson indicated that he expected conditions to become so difficult that small firms would be unable to obtain any raw materials. Despite later attempts by Congress to aid small manufacturers, some small businesses faced significant barriers to continued operations.[13]

Some clothing manufacturers managed to stay in operation by producing military uniforms for the men and women in the armed forces. Despite arguments that consolidation would make granting contracts easier, Dallas manufacturers profited from the large quantities of government contracts granted to Dallas companies. And these companies emerged from the war with new and modern plants.[14]

Page Boy and other Dallas manufacturers who were not making military goods managed to continue operations by obtaining some supplies, but the situation grew worse. In an attempt to tightly control the garment industry, Nelson took steps to centralize all clothing manufacturing in New York and the Northeast. By 1942 this step was damaging the Dallas market, and the Dallas Wholesalers and Manufacturers Association decided to file suit against the War Production Board. Under the direction of Lester Lorch, president of Lorch Company, the Dallas wholesalers obtained an injunction to prevent the centralization of wartime clothing manufacturing. This step eased the situation that Dallas manufacturers faced, but the garment industry still suffered under wartime regulations.[15]

Dallas merchant Stanley Marcus served as the apparel consultant to the War Production Board. In this position Marcus served as a liaison between the government regulators and the manufacturers. Marcus openly stressed the importance of conserving fabric and encouraged designers to simplify patterns. Additionally, he asked designers to create clothing that would be considered stylish through multiple seasons and would not go out of style over the next several years.[16] Marcus felt that even though the manufacturers were supplying the civilian market, it was their patriotic duty to help the war effort by conserving fabric.[17] Both Lester Lorch and Stanley Marcus were part of the Dallas Jewish community, and as such it is likely that Edna, Elsie, and Louise Frankfurt knew these men or their families. First, Stanley Marcus and Lester Lorch were only a few years older that Edna and Elsie Frankfurt. Second, it was likely that the families either attended the same temple or synagogue or they were members of the same clubs. Furthermore, many Jewish families lived in close proximity to each other, which made it easy to socialize with Jews who attended other congregations. Finally, even though Dallas was not a small city, most Jewish businessmen knew the other Jewish businessmen, and even if the families did not socialize together, they were part of one community.[18] Possibly the friendship between the Dallas manufacturers and those involved with government restrictions made it easier for the Dallas entrepreneurs to work with, or around, the regulations.

By the spring of 1943, revised regulation L-85 limited the "excessive use of fabrics" in the design and manufacture of all garments. This regulation imposed severe restrictions on all clothing designs. Collar and pocket sizes were regulated. Oversized collars were not allowed, and pockets could not be sewn on top of other fabric. Sleeves were regulated and both width and length prescribed; finally, the skirt width around the hips was limited. These restrictions dictated the wartime styles for women. This limitation made the Page Boy patented design even more important since it allowed Page Boy to create a comfortable design for a maternity skirt that obeyed the regulations. The suits or dresses had small collars and few pockets, and the skirts were mostly short and close fitting. In 1943 maternity designs came under government regulation for the first time. The new restrictions not only impacted designs, but they also impacted marketing. For example, no two garments could be priced as a unit, thus preventing a skirt and jacket from being sold as a unit (suit). Furthermore, war restrictions forced manufacturers to limit their wholesale distribution to firms that had previously been their customers—supposedly preventing expansion or growth and preventing new outlets from obtaining merchandise.[19]

During the war, according to Lois Rich-McCoy, who wrote about ten "self-made" women, including Elsie and Edna Frankfurt, Elsie Frankfurt told her sisters that she alone should travel to New York to purchase fabric and other needed supplies such as buttons. Rich-McCoy indicated that Elsie felt that her sisters would not pay the asking price for the fabric Page Boy needed to maintain production. Elsie contended that she was the only one who could deal with the suppliers, emphasizing that "you know what goes on in our world."[20]

During the war most Dallas garment manufacturers paid bribes to wholesalers and distributers in order to obtain enough fabric to continue manufacturing, reported Ralph Zeman, a longtime Dallas dress manufacturer.[21] It is highly likely, then, that Elsie made some payments to wholesalers that were not reflected on the books because Page Boy always managed to get enough fabric to continue to fill its orders.

Besides causing Louise, Edna, and Edna's family to return to Dallas, World War II forced other changes in Page Boy's marketing plans. Although the original outfits were sold as high-end fashions, by 1942 Sylvia Weaver, a writer for the *Los Angeles Times*, described budget items marketed by Page Boy. This line consisted of a four- to six-piece wardrobe that would take a woman from summer into fall; the total wardrobe only cost about twenty-two dollars. The average price for each of the six items was about four dollars, indicating that Page Boy was now marketing to all shoppers.[22] The prices reflected price, profit, and wage controls that were implemented during the war.

Despite the war restrictions Page Boy Manufacturing Company celebrated its fifth anniversary with a luncheon for its employees. During the past five years, the firm's production space had moved from the loft to a location at 1816-1/2 South Main and had grown from three employees to sixteen. However, Page Boy still maintained its retail shop in the Medical Arts Building, and five of the employees who were working in 1943 had been with the firm since the first year.[23] At the time of the luncheon, the firm employed one man, most likely the cutter, and fif-teen women; twelve were married and three unmarried. Furthermore, the company was now acting as both a wholesaler, with accounts in every state, and as a retailer, selling from their own shops.[24]

Demand remained strong, and production was able to grow despite the restrictions on manufacturing. Between the middle of 1943 and the middle of 1945, Page Boy placed few advertisements in the newspapers. Although it refrained from placing advertisements in the newspaper's fashion section, the company did advertise in the "help wanted" section of the *Dallas Morning News*. These advertisements appeared almost continually, beginning in the early months of 1943. Page Boy advertised for experienced operators capable of working on better dresses. Six months later they were still advertising for the same position—indicating that they were still shorthanded. By this time the firm was placing larger advertisements. In fact, one advertisement was written in verse:

> We like to work where it's a joy,
> You ought to see us at Page Boy,
> The rhythm of our power machines,
> Is set to music on the beam.
> We serve refreshments, prompt at three,
> Fruit juice and snacks, for energy,
> We pay as well as others do,
> Enough to buy a bond of two.
> For all the rest there is no fee.
> Come in and look around—That's free.[25]

As the war drew to a close, Page Boy resumed

advertising on a limited basis. The first advertisement appeared in the middle of 1945. Although some restrictions remained and some goods were in short supply, Page Boy began manufacturing a complete line of maternity garments by the end of the year. More significantly, within a few years Page Boy began receiving endorsement from fashion writers. Such columns served as unpaid advertisements and saved the company money. Fashion editors picked up information from Page Boy style shows or searched out photographs of Page Boy designs. Barbara Bundschu, a United Press fashion editor, wrote that even maternity clothing was manufactured with the newest spring styles in mind. "Three sisters from Dallas . . . showed off the newest collection of Page Boy maternity clothes for New Yorkers," she wrote. She elaborated that the styles included side-draped skirts, bare-shouldered evening gowns, and play suits; furthermore, each item was made from cotton, a cool fiber that allowed the fabric to breathe and the wearer to remain comfortable. She continued that the styles kept the lady comfortable with Page Boy "tricks," such as cut-out skirts with drawstrings that kept the hem in line, let-out pleats, and swimming suits with cover-up tops.[26]

With the war ending, Dallas manufacturers boosted their production, and Dallas became a center for sportswear design and women's clothing manufacturing. Moreover, the Dallas garment manufacturers became nationally recognized as leaders in the field of women's sportswear. According to Lester Lorch, longtime leader of the Dallas Manufacturers Association, this recognition was a reversal of earlier days in the Dallas garment trade. Prior to the war, stores carrying Dallas-made clothing often removed the labels from the Dallas goods because the retailers believed that Dallas labels decreased the value of garments. Additionally, according to Lorch, many high-end stores had not wanted to sell garments that had manufacturer's labels sewn into the garment. Instead, they preferred to sell garments with store labels suggesting that the garments were originals or made for that individual shop.[27]

In the midst of the war, Southern Methodist University had made plans to establish a new school of design, but implementation was slow. After the war the pent-up demand for new clothing contributed to the explosive growth of all the women's apparel manufacturers in Dallas.[28] As a sign of their strong financial position, the largest Dallas manufacturers, including Page Boy, contributed to the new design program at Southern Methodist University. The dedication, which was held at the Adolphus Hotel, drew more than 250 retailers and manufacturers to hear E. P. Simmons, the president of Sanger Bros, L. P. Lorch, president of the Dallas Fashion and Sportswear Association, and W. C. Stetson, merchandising manager of women's apparel at Marshall Field's of Chicago, speak about the Dallas fashion industry. Stetson described the Dallas market, saying, "Dallas' dressy dresses, suits, coats, junior misses' apparel and children's wear, all of distinctive quality and workmanship" are found "in all sections of the country," and "[t]he Dallas market

Edna, Elsie, and Louise after World War II, ca. 1947

and the new school of design show America's determination to give a good account of itself in the post-war world whose marketing schemes and schedules will be made immeasurably shorter by fast airplane transportation and improved communication." With these lofty predictions and a warning that the "war emergency has somewhat sidetracked" the development of women's fashions, the speakers predicted that SMU's school of design would further stimulate the development of design in the region.[29]

Although the Frankfurt sisters of Page Boy participated in the manufacturers' activities, their firm differed from most Dallas firms. The sisters had created a distinctive model for their firm. The owners did not use middlemen or jobbers to market their designs; instead, they sold directly to retail customers in Page Boy's shops or wholesaled their own designs.[30] Moreover, Page Boy's owners and managers were young women and thus were unique among other manufacturers in Texas. These differences cre-

ated boundaries and to some extent limited the owners' interactions with other merchandisers in Dallas.[31] In an article titled "Dallas-Born Idea Grows into
National Business," the author began, "Two little
Dallas spinsters and their married sister have par-
layed a $500 nest egg and some mathematical prin-
ciples into the nationally-known Page Boy maternity
wear business."[32] Surprisingly, these "spinsters"
were only about 25 and 35, and despite being women
they were hard-driving businesswomen with about
250 active accounts.[33]

In 1947 Dallas fashion writer Gay Simpson referred to older maternity styles as the "ill-fitting
dresses that hiked up in front" when she noted that
back in 1938 Page Boy had "solved fashion perplexities for thousands of the nation's mothers." Simpson claimed that Page Boy sold 10,000 of the original style during the first year because there was a
"crying need for a fashionable and becoming maternity dress." She also noted that, with the end of fabric rationing, designs had changed. Skirts were longer and used more fabric, and some had drapes or
flounces integrated into the new designs. New Page
Boy designs also included sequins and bright colors
in pure silk and woolens—fabrics that had been ra-
tioned during the war. Faille and taffeta, fabrics that
stood away from the body and made a crisper design
statement, were also used generously. Finally, Simpson mentioned that sophisticated mothers-to-be
could find any type of dress they required, from dark
crepe dinner dresses to hostess pajamas and even
sporty dresses. She wrote, "The teen-ager can have

MATERNITY FASHIONS
by
Page Boy
DALLAS, TEXAS

STORK CLUB
February 18, 1947

Cover of program for Stork Club style show, 1947

her dark gabardine pepped up with sparkling stripes or checked wool boxy coats over slim skirts." Simpson wrote that all the styles were adjustable and comfortable and could be found in Page Boy stores in Dallas, Los Angeles, San Francisco, and Indianapolis, as well as in many department store outlets around the country. These new styles introduced a new drawstring adjustment and a hook system to allow the waist to expand.[34]

The Frankfurt sisters clearly sought publicity that would promote themselves and the business. With her usual flair for the dramatic, Elsie convinced Sherman Billingsley, owner and manager of the Stork Club, a New York City night club favored by celebrities, to allow Page Boy to schedule a style show in his main dining room.[35] After all, what better place to show maternity clothing than the Stork Club?

The event was scheduled for February 18, 1947, and with a location and date selected, Elsie found six models or "mannequins," who flawlessly marched down the runway, showing off the Page Boy styles. Invitations were extended to special guests and fashion writers. One of the models was six months pregnant, and the ladies attending the fashion show played a guessing game trying to figure out which one it was. The Page Boy designs included multipart mix-and-match skirts, pants, and vests, dramatic palazzo pants, conservative suits, and shorts with cover-up tops. A few of the styles reflected an Asian influence, featuring a mandarin jacket with gold braid over a black crepe, slit dinner skirt. This "soci-

Nightie shown
at the Stork Club, 1947

ety-wise style show" exemplified Elsie's knack for the dramatic and became a model for future publicity. While the write up about the fashion show mentioned the adjustable skirt with the drawstring waistline, it also mentioned that some of the skirts used drapes that could be adjusted, similar to a wraparound skirt. The review also mentioned that Page Boy had reached a volume of a million dollars a year, thereby touting the firm's growth.[36] This style show was billed as "Maternity Fashions by Page Boy under the direction of Elsie Miller Davis." Adrienne Ames

Edna, Elsie, and Louise holding storks donated to the Dallas zoo, 1947

Louise to Charles Gartner. No date for the wedding was announced. Clearly the wedding must have been a quiet affair because eight months later Benjamin died after a long illness, and the obituary listed Louise as Mrs. Charles Gartner.[37]

Shortly before the end of the decade, Edna, Elsie, and Louise made a splash in the Dallas newspapers when they donated a pair of full-grown storks to the Dallas zoo. The *Dallas Morning News* focused on the event and carried a picture of zoo administrator Walton Carlton alongside the three smartly dressed sisters holding the beaks of two storks. The caption noted that the storks had just flown in from California and that the sisters were donating them to the Marsalis Park Zoo.[38] Photographs were also taken of the three women with the storks in front of the Page Boy Factory.

After the war ended, pregnancy rates skyrocketed and dress sales soared. As production grew the sisters needed additional help managing the manufacturing aspect of the business. Thirty-six-year-old Abe Ravkind, Edna's husband, had entered the army in November of 1943, and upon his return in 1946, the sisters hired him as a production manager. Page Boy now employed 100 people—still mostly women. In 1948 *Time* magazine ran a short article about the firm, calling it a "merchandising sensation." Although the business remained a private concern, at various times claims about its sales figures and profits became public, and the *Time* article reported that the sisters grossed about $1,026,584 and netted about ten percent of that amount.[39]

served as the commentator; the models were supplied by Powers and Company, and accessories were provided by Best and Company.

Shortly after the sisters returned from New York on April 13, 1947, Ben and Jenny Frankfurt announced the approaching marriage of their daughter

Edna, Elsie, and Louise inspecting design proposals for new plant, 1947

Edna, Elsie, and Louise during construction, 1948–1949

blueprint for Page Boy's actions but the formula for its success.[40]

With the increase in sales, Page Boy outgrew its manufacturing space. Considering all their alternatives, the sisters decided to have a new plant built, one that was designed specifically for their needs. Edna, Elsie, and Louise searched for a site and enthusiastically purchased land north of downtown Dallas. This location was close to many new medical offices, so they again placed their outlet close to where potential customers would see the shop. But when the sisters began to plan the building they took a step backward. Building costs had risen after the war, so they hesitated. A few days after Edna traveled to California to be present for the opening of the second shop in the Los Angeles area, Elsie called Edna, asking if they should begin building. Edna said, "Maybe not yet." But a few days later, when the temperature in Dallas hit 104 degrees, Elsie called again to announce that she was going ahead with their plans to start the new building. Then she added emphatically that the new plant was going to be air-conditioned.

As midcentury arrived Page Boy and the Frankfurt sisters became recognized celebrities. In fact, one article in the *Dallas Morning News* touted, "Page Boy Trademark Known Coast to Coast." This article quoted Elsie, who said that the business formula was simple: see "a need, design something to fill it, and build" the business as you go. Elsie quipped, "Any idea, basically sound, with the proper publicity can be built into a big business." She added, "Of course, the product must be the best there is." For the next few decades this statement became not only the

Back in Dallas the sisters hired architect George Dahl and builder J. E. Morgan & Son from El Paso to design and build the structure, which would include space for the plant, office, and showroom all in the same building. In August of 1949, Page Boy opened its new headquarters located at Cedar Springs and Olive Street.[41] The long, streamlined building typical of midcentury modern architecture consisted of two floors. All the manufacturing facilities, containing

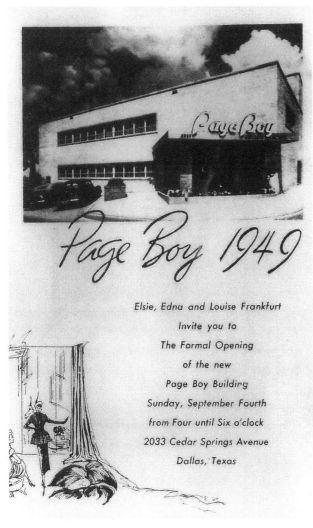

Page Boy 1949

Elsie, Edna and Louise Frankfurt

Invite you to

The Formal Opening

of the new

Page Boy Building

Sunday, September Fourth

from Four until Six o'clock

2033 Cedar Springs Avenue

Dallas, Texas

Invitation to opening of new factory and showroom, 1949

both the cutting tables and rows of sewing machines, were located on the second floor. The first floor contained the showroom at one end of the building and all the offices at the other. These sections were connected by a long hall that also included space for the telephone operator and switchboard. The hall was decorated with mirrors, and the offices were light and glitzy. Elsie and Edna shared a large office with two extra-large desks, and Louise had her own office. Neither as fancy nor as large as her sisters' office, it was planned to accommodate Louise's designing needs and even had space for an assistant. She also had storage niches for fabric, trims, buttons, and a padded dress form. Brenda Berg, Louise's older daughter, remembers the entire building, upstairs and down, as a bright, cheerful, and exciting space to visit.[42]

After the war Elsie Frankfurt began making regular trips to New York, and by 1950 she was spending many weeks each year away from Dallas. While in New York she rented an apartment in the Pierre Hotel, considering the hotel her home in New York. During these trips she left Edna and Louise to run the Dallas operation. Elsie also traveled to and from California where Page Boy had just opened a shop in San Francisco. In addition to the general office and the factory, the new building housed a library containing information about maternal and baby care and a new larger showroom so the styles could be shown to buyers in comfort and luxury. The larger plant allowed the firm to increase the number of employees by about fifty percent, and this expansion al-

Louise, Edna, and Elsie at opening of new facilities, 1949

tention indicated that the Dallas business community recognized the significance of the Frankfurt sisters and the importance of Page Boy manufacturing to the Dallas business environment. Page Boy's important milestone was also reported in the *New York Times*.[45]

Most of the press releases claimed that Elsie alone represented Page Boy at wholesale shows and in New York. However, according to Louise, she herself also traveled around the country, making many sales calls and carrying a suitcase filled with Page Boy samples. She explained that she worked as a sales representative, showing off Page Boy designs to buyers for large department stores in various cities. Her contribution as a sales representative for the business was never acknowledged in the press.[46]

Page Boy introduced another innovation as styles changed. By now the company had added many one-piece garments to the original line of two-piece suits. To make some designs function as stylish maternity garments for women in the early months of pregnancy as well as the later months, and even for nonpregnant women, the sisters began inserting hidden zippers into the skirts and dresses. The zippers could be opened to expand the width of the waist. These outfits could be used as maternity clothing when the zippers were unzipped, and after the baby arrived women could convert the dresses or skirts back to regular ready-to-wear by zipping the zippers closed. Being able to convert a maternity dress or skirt back to a normal dress or skirt provided a woman with a stylish outfit while she were pregnant and an outfit that could also be worn after deliv-

lowed Page Boy to also increase production by about fifty percent. During this time each of the sisters had developed an interest in promoting good health and exercise, and they designed a workers' exercise area in the building.[43] Neiman Marcus Galleries was hired to design and decorate the showrooms, offices, and the new Dallas shop. Selecting Neiman Marcus to decorate the spaces suggests that the company was again marketing to the affluent customer. When the building was complete, Dallas mayor Wallace Savage cut the ribbon at the formal opening, and the sisters were feted at Brook Hollow Country Club by National City Bank president DeWitt Ray.[44] Such atery, when she had perhaps not returned to her prepregnancy size or had less money to spend on herself.[47] Page Boy could market the dresses and outfits as clothing that could work in both situations, and women could thereby justify spending more on maternity clothing than they might have originally planned since they could continue to wear the outfits after delivery.

Writers sought Elsie Frankfurt for interviews, and Louise's name now appeared in advertisements as Page Boy's designer. Nevertheless, the sisters were still women and as such were subjected to the prejudices of the time—even in their own hometown. The war had slowed the implementation of the new design program at SMU, but shortly after the war ended the university began work on establishing the program. SMU celebrated the program's third anniversary in 1950 and invited local manufacturers and business owners, including the Frankfurt sisters to speak to the classes. Topics ranged from advertising to marketing and managerial problems. However, Edna, Elsie, and Louise were singled out, and the planners requested that they speak to the groups about secretarial training.[48] This request demonstrates that, even in their hometown, the owners of Page Boy were still seen as women first and as entrepreneurs and business professionals second.

Short sleeve, two-piece suit with reverse pleats in jacket and skirt, white collar and large clear buttons closing jacket

Two-piece suit, white jacket with Asian-inspired embroidery on left shoulder

Embroidered scallop detail in a pastel-colored cotton dress with self-covered buttons, hook adjustments at waist

Right, mandarin collar, navy-and-beige rayon shantung dress with Chinese dragon embroidery in gold and brilliant colors, asymmetrical buttons on right side

Vertical inserts of white eyelet embroidery on the bodice of pale-yellow poplin dress, drawstring adjustment

Vertical-and-horizontal striped dress with tie waist and bows on cap sleeves

Afternoon dress of pure silk, pen and ink print, cap-sleeved with drawstring adjustment at waist

Green-and-beige striped washable dress with set-in sleeves and large pockets, removable belt to be used early in pregnancy or after baby arrives, $17.95

Dark-colored dress with white eyelet trim and matching satin ribbons threaded in eyelet, removable belt

Playsuit in solid and striped denim, shorts in solid color, adjustable at waist and boy-cut stripe shirt

Afternoon dress of lime San Chu deluxe rayon crepe with keyhole neckline, embroidered neckline with gold flecks and hook adjustment skirt

Crepe afternoon dresses, both with cap sleeves and striped inserts in skirts

Coral crepe jerkin, front quilted with rhinestone buttons, with short skirt or long skirt, two pieces, $39.95; full-sleeved crepe blouse, $25.00

Coral crepe jerkin over slacks

Appliquéd box jacket over slacks or skirt for an interchangeable suit

Navy slacks paired with a red coat with side slits; on the right side a white yoke continues to the back, $25.00

Embroidered yoke and pockets on playsuit with harem pants

Evening outfit with sequin design across the shoulders, belted or unbelted.

Swing jacket with asymmetrical button closing running from collar to underarm,
three-quarters sleeve, and Page Boy's fitted skirt.

Box jacket with white collar and tailored bow at the chin with Page Boy's fitted skirt

Twin styles: front is a two-piece suit with swing jacket, color boxes with inserts or white and light colors; back model wears dress in similar style.

Airy light champagne-blonde chiffon skirt with reembroidered lace bodice

Left: Emerald green taffeta creates a floating evening coat with black fox cuffs
Right: Emerald green taffeta dress under the coat forms a tunic dress with Empire-cut
top and slim Page Boy cut-out skirt

Long two-piece evening suit with shawl collar and tent bottom

Simple black dress, short-sleeved tent-style top over Page Boy fitted skirt

Ski outfit with white top and slim pants

Model on right wearing front-pleat dress in red jersey with airy camouflage-red chiffon detachable skirt. Jayne Meadows on left wearing weaning coat of embroidered satin with mandarin collar

Jayne Meadows with (left to right) Louise Frankfurt Gartner, Elsie Frankfurt, and Edna Frankfurt Ravkind

Jayne Meadows with group of models

Chapter 3

A Decade of Accomplishments, Acknowledgments, and Ambition

During the last three years of the 1940s, Page Boy's income increased between twenty and forty percent each year. The company's sales surpassed the million-dollar mark during 1947, and in 1948 sales rose 21.5 percent over the 1947 figure. For the first nine months of 1949, sales had already risen another 32 percent over the previous year. After the new plant came online, Page Boy was turning out between 1,200 and 1,400 garments each week. This was a 40 percent increase in production over its output prior to moving. Even at this pace, however, Page Boy was barely able to fill its regular orders. Sales manager Bill Moser said that, because of the high demand from its standing customers, Page Boy was hesitant to accept any new accounts. Furthermore, he indicated that the new sales outlet in Dallas would serve as the firm's test marketing store. Page Boy would make a few garments in a new style and offer them for sale in the Dallas outlet. If new styles sold well from the Dallas store, Page Boy would move the styles into standard production and out across the country. In 1950 Page Boy owned five shops in addition to the two it maintained in Dallas.[1] Three were located in California: one in Beverly Hills, one in Los Angeles, and one in San Francisco. The company had one store in Indianapolis and another new store in Cleveland. Besides its own specialty stores, Page Boy had outlets in many department stores, including Lord & Taylor, Saks, Marshall Field's, Foley Brothers, Kerr's, and Maison Blanche in New Orleans. These department stores added another 350 outlets to Page Boy's distribution.

In approximately 1950 Page Boy focused on "sleek, chic," high-fashion, well-made garments with prices ranging from $15 to over $100. Realizing that some women might not want to spend or, as Elsie said, "invest," in purchasing such upscale maternity clothing, Page Boy began making "convertible" dresses and suits. These outfits came with insets that could be sewn in the skirts to cover the front opening when the woman was no longer pregnant. In fact, sales of some of these garments were made to women who were not pregnant. When buyers asked Elsie why she did not add a line of regular ready-to-wear clothes to the Page Boy name, Elsie said she "was quite content making the finest maternity dresses in the U.S." and only wanted to grow slowly. Despite the limited scope of their designs, the sales for 1950 were "up 1,500% over the $100,000 sales volume from Page Boy's first full year in operation, 1939."[2]

By midcentury Elsie claimed that she lived part-time in New York so that she could be available for all the major showings. She loved the exciting life she found in New York, and although she favored a slow growth for Page Boy, she and her sisters expanded production lines and added lingerie and sportswear to the standard maternity suits and dress outfits they sold. Page Boy continued to expand the scope of its marketing, and it reached out to potential customers who otherwise might not have had access to a Page Boy shop or a department store carrying the Page Boy line. To promote sales to stay-at-home mothers, the company published a free catalogue that displayed all of its styles. These items could be ordered through the California shop.[3] This step broadened the customer base to include not only professional women and affluent mothers but also stay-at home mothers and women from smaller communities.

Although all the sisters made public appearances and loved traveling, Elsie, as the only single sister, traveled to Europe to visit various European fashion houses in order to see for herself the latest high-fashion designs. She also began a love affair with couture clothing and began collecting designer outfits that she treasured all her life. Elsie's travels sparked a fascination with historical styles and maternity fashions that culminated in Page Boy's commissioning of costumed dolls, each wearing a replica of a maternity fashion from an earlier era. The costumes represented styles beginning with a chemise worn in ancient Egypt and a stola worn in both classical Greece and Rome. Several dolls wore costumes representing styles popular in medieval Europe, and at least two costumes represented nineteenth-century dresses. One doll represented a modern woman and was outfitted in a replica of a current Page Boy design. Numerous articles describing the dolls appeared in newspapers, and *Vogue* publicized them in an article, "Quick History of Maternity Fashions," printed in its October 1950 issue. Elsie was even photographed sitting on the floor with the dolls scattered around her. According to Louise Gartner, the dolls were Elsie's idea, and it is not clear how much research was done to investigate the authenticity of the garments created for the dolls. For example, the Egyptian doll's garment depicted clothing worn by a figure drawn on the wall of an

Egyptian temple. Whether or not the picture represented a pregnant woman is uncertain, but Elsie claimed that the fashion could have served a pregnant woman. Furthermore, although the dolls were dressed in styles that were popular at various times, it is questionable whether they actually represented maternity clothing of that era or not. Another doll wears a "maternity dress" supposedly worn by Empress Josephine of France. This design, called Empire style, was popular in the early nineteenth century and was made fashionable by Josephine and her friends, who wore it as everyday fashion—not necessarily as maternity clothing. Nevertheless, the dolls served their purpose: to draw attention to maternity fashion and specifically to the Page Boy line. The dolls appeared in Lord & Taylor's window alongside Page Boy fashions, and they traveled around the country, promoting Page Boy clothing wherever they appeared. Despite their lack of authenticity, the dolls served as an advertising gimmick to bring attention to Page Boy itself.[4]

Page Boy commissioned two sets of the dolls. Each doll traveled in a miniature trunk made by Eagle Lock Company of Terryville, Connecticut. The black metal trunks were about ten inches wide, twenty-six inches long, and ten inches deep. Each was made especially to hold one doll. They had braces at the bottom where the feet fit and at the head, and there were ties around the body of the doll to keep it from moving around in the trunk. Each doll was packed with tissue paper and excelsior when it was shipped. Elsie called the figurines "dolls," but

Elsie holding maternity dolls, ca. 1952

more than likely they were miniature mannequins made from a composite material. After the dolls had traveled around to various stores, they began to deteriorate and were donated to the Texas Fashion Institute. Edward Hoyenski, the collection manager of the Texas Fashion Collection, believes that probably Elsie contacted one of the companies that supplied Page Boy's mannequins and asked the company to make the miniature mannequins for Page Boy. The legs and bodies were formed as one piece and were hollow as if liquid plaster or composite had been poured into a mold. The arms were created in vari-

Dolls in the window of Lord & Taylor, ca. 1952

ous positions and were attached to the body with elastic bands that crossed from one arm to another inside the chest of the figure. The tension from the elastic held the arms in the sockets and allowed the arms to be moved. Some figures had applied hair, and others had hair formed as part of the head. They all had similar features with eyes, eyebrows, and mouth painted onto the face. Each doll had its own stand with two dowels extending up from the base for about five inches. The dowels fit into the hollow feet and legs.[5] The dolls and the publicity they created became another way that Page Boy drew attention to itself. Although Page Boy paid for the creation of the dolls and the transportation of the trunks, it received free publicity wherever they were displayed.

Louise Frankfurt had married Charles Gartner in 1947, and her first child arrived in 1948. The mere fact that one of the Frankfurt sisters was expecting became the subject of celebrity gossip. Syndicated columnist Leonard Lyons, who wrote the column "Broadway Melody" for the *New York Times* and other papers, announced that "in Dallas next week the youngest of the Frankfurt sisters will have a baby." Along with this announcement he mentioned that the firm would be presenting its fall collection that same week.[6] Lyons's musings also appeared in the *Washington Post*. In that column he again mentioned that one of the Frankfurt sisters was going to have a baby. Although all three of the sisters were becoming celebrities, Elsie, who was single and spent much of her time either in New York or on the West Coast, became the most visible sister.

They

didn't

believe

her . . .

But seeing is believing. Mrs. Louise Frankfurt Gartner, wearing one of her own designs, photographed last July leaving her designer office at Page Boy for the hospital and the arrival (some five hours later) of her baby son. Louise, one of Page Boy's three famous Frankfurt sisters, is proof that today's modern mother, modern maternity fashions are more beautiful than ever.

PAGE BOY . . . *fall and winter 1952*

Pregnant Louise pictured in Page Boy catalog, 1951–1952

When Louise became pregnant again in 1951, her name not only appeared in advertisements, but her likeness also appeared in sketches as a model for some of her own maternity creations. In one *Los Angeles Times* advertisement for a three-piece suit including skirt, slacks, and jacket, the copy began, "A designer designs her own wardrobe while she awaits her baby—the result is maternity clothes with a flair, plus versatility, plus comfort." The illustration displayed a smart double-breasted jacket in beige over dark slacks or skirt. The later items came in navy, brown, and black. This outfit was designed not with the usual oval cut-out in the skirt and pants but with a concealed zipper and tie in the front center. The zipper allowed the waist to expand as needed, and the tie held the garments in place. The jacket sold for $22.95 and the skirt and slacks for $12.95 and $14.95 respectively.[7]

That same month *Good Housekeeping* magazine featured Louise in an article titled "When the Designer Has a Baby." This three-page spread showcased Louise modeling several outfits that sold for fifteen dollars to thirty dollars. One was a dinner suit with a velveteen jacket and long skirt. The skirt was also shown with a light-colored brocade top. The jacket sleeves were cut wide with a large rolled cuff. Another outfit consisted of a faille suit trimmed in velveteen. Louise wore the suit with a dotted blouse that had a large tie collar that could be brought through a loop at the neck of the jacket. The three outfits (the one shown in the *Los Angeles Times* advertisement and the two in the *Good Housekeeping* arti-cle) were designed using extravagant amounts of fabric. One had large patch pockets; another sported large rolled cuffs, and the blouse had fluffy ties. The design of these costumes that used extra fabric illustrated the fashion backlash to the restrictions that had been in place during the war years.[8]

During the late 1940s and the 1950s either Louise or Elsie were always given credit for the Page Boy designs; then years later as Elsie recounted the Page Boy history, she took credit as the designer, and Louise was left out of the story. However, one article printed in a commercial newsletter in approximately 1954 mentioned that Page Boy had hired three designers, all "college-trained," to assist with the designing. This article indicated that Louise and the three women created all the designs and produced about fifty completed sample garments for each of the three seasons.[9]

Edna, Elsie, and Louise were energetic, photogenic, and smart. They not only sought attention for themselves, but writers also sought them out as experts on fashion and business. However, because Elsie was the president, she often served as the spokesperson for Page Boy. In 1951 the Young Presidents' Organization announced that it would admit its first woman, Elsie Frankfurt.[10] Female newspaper columnists announced this accomplishment in stories that appeared across the nation from New York City and Niagara Falls, New York, to Cedar Rapids, Michigan, Dallas, Galveston, Texas, and across to the West Coast, to Los Angeles and San Mateo, California. One columnist wrote that when Elsie walked into the ballroom of the Prince George Hotel for the luncheon and formal induction, the 220 assembled businessmen did not believe that she was their new colleague. The members had all voted by mail, based on the firm's business credentials, and none of them had ever seen or met Elsie Frankfurt before she arrived for the meeting. They were stunned as she stood before them and told the Page Boy story.[11] Even though the YPO had admitted a young woman, the press release noted that it had admitted its first "girl."

Membership in the organization was restricted in several ways. First, new members were all selected by a vote of the current membership. Second, to be considered for membership, a prospective member had to be the president of a business having more than $1 million in annual gross revenue; and third, the nominee had to be under the age of forty. In all the articles about her achievement, Elsie Frankfurt claimed to be only thirty-three at the time she became a member, but in fact she had turned forty the year she was inducted into the organization. Although Elsie's age was incorrect, more than likely her assertion that Page Boy took in annual revenues of more than $2 million was true.[12]

Ever eager to sharpen her management skills, Elsie Frankfurt always enrolled in additional seminars offered through the Harvard graduate school of business administration and sponsored by the Young Presidents' Organization. After leaving one seminar, she traveled to New York to check on the showroom and meet with clients. While in New York she was photographed with Errol Flynn's third wife, Patrice Wymore. Mrs. Flynn was being outfitted with a Page Boy wardrobe for a trip to Rome where she was to meet her husband. Never shy of using any form of publicity, Edna had the photographs sent out as press releases, but of course, they served as advertisements also.[13] This became a standard practice for Page Boy, and for many years the company continued to have actresses photographed in their clothes.[14]

As the president and face of Page Boy, Elsie continued to be the focus of attention. That same year she was recognized as one of the "Young Women of the Year" by *Mademoiselle* magazine. The award was made to nine women who were recognized for achieving "distinctive records in their fields." The list of honorees included, among others, dancer Maria Tallchief, a native American and the first American woman recognized as a prima ballerina; tennis star Maureen Connolly; mathematician Ilse Novak of Princeton, New Jersey; and actresses Maureen Stapleton and Shelley Winters.[15]

In 1951 Elsie also attended an executive seminar at Harvard along with a few other members of the Young Presidents' Club. True to her personality she forcefully responded to one of the speakers, who commented that most women in business only remained in business temporarily—until they married or had children. Elsie sharply rebuked him, saying that such a statement was only true "in storybooks." She continued, "A baby means only a couple of months away from the job. More and more women are going into every field of business and the professions." Volunteering her own opinion about this situation, she stated that many of those women were staying in the work force because they had to work. Yet although she was outspoken and never hesitated to speak her mind about women's roles or the business world, Elsie remained very feminine. She looked like a petite debutante, and like one, she meticulously planned her wardrobe so that she could wear a different outfit each day of the seminar. During an interview after the seminars were complete, she proudly proclaimed to a reporter, "I didn't repeat once."[16]

Elsie was a whirlwind of activity during 1950 and 1951. Even though she spent much of her time away from Dallas, in early 1951 she was asked to serve on the executive committee of the Women's Division of the Jewish Welfare Federation campaign. She agreed to serve and worked for the campaign, which pledged to raise $1 million for the United Jewish Appeal and fifty other Jewish relief organizations. That she was approached to serve on this committee demonstrates that she still maintained a strong connection with Dallas and its Jewish community.[17]

By the beginning of 1952, Louise's preference for separates had become evident in many of the styles manufactured by Page Boy, and these styles were also seen in designs made by other manufacturers. The new designs shifted away from matching suits and dresses to more casual mix-and-match styles made of coordinating, but not necessarily matching fabric. Additionally, new sporty fabrics were replacing some of the more formal fabrics such as faille, crepe, and worsted that Page Boy had favored during its first decade in operation. Denim and polished cotton began to appear in Page Boy's more casual everyday fashions. These casual styles and fabrics allowed mothers-to-be to purchase individual pieces they liked and then combine them in outfits they thought appropriate. Mix-and-match garments increased the number of outfits a woman had available in her closet while decreasing the actual number of garments she needed to buy.

Although the styles were changing, Page Boy still manufactured clothing for the professional woman and continued to focus on her needs. Page Boy offered suits with two skirts or a skirt with two jackets so that the ensembles could work as a three-way convertible ensemble. Each garment was sold separately, and all were made of complementary or matching fabrics. Page Boy also began to sell more single pieces, and even the suit pieces were sold individually, similar to the way garments had been marketed during the war. Barbara Brady, the New York correspondent for the *Dallas Morning News,* wrote a column about maternity fashions and named several manufacturers, including Lane Bryant and Page Boy. Although Lane Bryant had continued to manufacture some maternity garments, they were primarily marketed as lower-end items. By 1952 a few other companies were competing with Page Boy in the upscale maternity market. Stork Styles, owned by Ben Goldwasser, specialized in wraparound skirts and tops, which it manufactured and wholesaled to

Secret strategy by PAGE BOY, clever as the Chinese themselves. (left) Style 6 skirt, horizontal zipper allows invisible expansion. Sizes 10-18. Black, brown, navy rayon faille or gabardine. **12.95** Grey or brown flannel. **17.95** (Right) Style 3, window cut-out skirt . . . most comfortable maternity skirt devised, patented by PAGE BOY. Sizes 10-18. Black, brown, navy rayon crepe or gabardine **12.95**. Also, long black crepe cut-out skirt, for evening. Style 5. **22.95**

New skirt designs from Page Boy catalog, 1951

specialty stores. By this time there were nearly 100 manufacturers in the United States wholesaling maternity garments and about 500 specialty shops focusing on supplying the maternity market. This number did not include department stores that also carried maternity clothing.[18] Moreover, most of these other manufacturers could not compete with Page Boy's fitted skirt because the original design was patented. However, styles were changing, and even Page Boy was experimenting with alternate solutions to the skirt problem. The expansive growth in the number of maternity clothing manufacturers and outlets was a reflection of the increased birthrate.

Louise continued to appear in advertisements and in photographs wearing the designs she had created. Although some of the outfits were mix-and-match, a few were dressy, and she even designed one dinner suit with fur trim on the sleeves. Furthermore, she appeared in the Page Boy catalog. The caption announced, "They didn't believe her," saying that the picture had been taken when she left the office on the way to deliver her son.[19]

By 1950 style guidelines and fabric restrictions were a thing of the past. But the business expansion that took place after the end of World War II created other problems, including swiftly rising prices. Page Boy printed this message on the back page of its fall and winter 1952 brochure. "No price for any article shown herein exceeds the ceiling price for that article, as determined under the application of the OPS ceiling regulation." This note referred to the Office

56

Pregnant Louise modeling dinner suit
trimmed in fur, 1951

Design drawing of dinner suit trimmed in fur, 1950s

of Price Stabilization, a governmental agency created to write guidelines and rules that regulated prices
and prevented excessive inflation during the Korean
War.[20]

Emphasizing the new attitude about separates,
Page Boy marketed a "planned" mix-and-match
wardrobe. This wardrobe could appeal to the stay-at-

home mother or the young woman with limited funds. The wardrobe included a skirt that could be worn snugly around the waist and then expanded with the zippers that opened to allow additional fabric gussets to cover the waist. The skirt was offered in grey, Kelly green, and red. Additional items in this wardrobe included a two-piece all-occasion suit with a detachable collar, manufactured in black, navy, and gray, a short-sleeve white blouse that could be worn with any of the skirts, a top in pastel colors with rhinestone buttons, and one additional blouse to match the skirts. Furthermore, Page Boy offered a detachable collar and cuffs for the previously mentioned blouse and extra tops, including a sleeveless top in plaid that could be worn alone or over the white blouse. Finally, they offered a red, lime-green, or white double-breasted jacket that could be worn both as a maternity top or after the baby was born. While prices for the items ranged from $1.95 for the detachable collar and cuffs to $29.95 for the suit, the cost of the entire wardrobe averaged about $12.50 per month paid out over eight months.[21]

Continuing their emphasis on casual wear, Louise Gartner designed clothing that included play clothes and even swimsuits for pregnant women. She designed one play suit / bathing suit outfit from permanent finish chintz. The outfit included wide-leg shorts with a jersey brief attached at the waist, enabling the wearer to use the garment as a bathing suit that could actually go into the water. The halter top with built-in bra buttoned to the shorts in the front but also sported removable straps. The matching cover-up was sleeveless but cut with an inverted pleat in the back so the halter top could be removed and the cover-up worn as a long overblouse with just the shorts.[22]

Like many department stores Page Boy created semiannual brochures that advertised its latest fashions. But unlike other firms Page Boy treated its brochures more like magazines for pregnant women; they even used the term "magazine" in the title: "Page Boy Fashion Magazine for Smart Young Mothers-to-be." Page Boy included information about the evolution of its styles. When it started manufacturing maternity clothes, it pointed out, it had only offered sets, but it soon began making extra tops for suits; those had evolved into a line of separates and then mix-and-match. One section written by Herman Kantor, M.D., an assistant professor of obstetrics and gynecology at the University of Texas, even included information and suggestions about healthy eating and admonished pregnant women not to eat "everything in sight." The article also suggested that the women drink a quart of milk a day and not drink whiskey. These recommendations were written in rhyme and continued, "Becky has a headache—and her back is hurting too, Poor Becky's feet are swollen so—She can't put on her shoe. Becky is in misery—can her liver be at fault? No! Becky's only trouble is she uses TOO MUCH SALT!" Six more pages were devoted to exercise, weight control, and what was considered a moderate diet, including skimmed milk and foods with iron to prevent anemia. These health suggestions were quite forward looking for their day and reflected how health conscious the sisters were.

Evidently Page Boy collaborated with David Evans, maker of women's shoes, because the magazine included an advertisement for low- and medium-heel shoes that were appropriate for pregnant women. The publication illustrated eight shoe styles were deemed appropriate and indicated that all the information came from "Shoe News by David Evans." The lengthy magazine included about ten pages of text and also the latest Page Boy designs. The separates offered in the booklet ran from $12.95 to $69.95 and $89.95 for two suits. But the cover suit, which was created of Forstmann's cashmere soft 100% virgin wool and had a ranch mink collar and cuffs, sold for $150.

That same year another edition of the magazine contained pictures of Page Boy clothes and mothers' health tips along with a several pages devoted to "Stork League Hollywood U.S.A." These pages were filled with stories about Hollywood families who were expecting babies during the spring of 1953. It is not clear whether all the women named were customers of Page Boy, but some were described wearing Page Boy clothes. For example, "Elizabeth Taylor was all aglow with her first pregnancy when she shopped at the Page Boy's Beverly Hills establishment." The article continued, "Recent shoppers in Page Boy's Wilshire Boulevard branch included Lucille Ball, and Mrs. Jack Webb; at Page Boy's Beverly Hills shop we glimpsed such movie and TV names as Jane Powell, Marie McDonald, Jo Stafford, Mrs.

Mario Lanza, Shelly Winters, Elizabeth Taylor, Gloria Henry, Barbara Rush, Jane Nigh and the beloved Judy Garland." The article mentioned other women who were pregnant at the time that the article went to press, but it was not clear whether they had also purchased Page Boy clothes. From these articles it is clear that Page Boy wanted to educate the women they clothed, but they were not above indicating that their customers could dress like a star in Page Boy outfits.[23]

Consumption increased, raising sales figures for all businesses. During the first few years of the 1950s, the Dallas apparel industry contributed about $15 million annually to the Dallas economy. Moreover, most of the manufacturing companies were expanding and were outgrowing the available office and workroom space in downtown Dallas. According to both Louise Frankfurt Gartner and Ralph Zeman, many of the Dallas manufacturers had also outgrown the pool of workers located within an easy commute of the near downtown plants. The need for new factories and the lack of an adequate workforce spurred a move to the suburbs or to surrounding communities such as Lancaster, McKinney, and Waxahachie. Because Page Boy had moved north of the downtown area in 1949, it did not need to move farther out. However, it and the other apparel manufacturers located around Dallas substantially contributed to the Dallas economy. First the Dallas firms grew their markets, and then they also expanded the number of seasonal or thematic markets presented by the Dallas manufacturers. As the Dallas market matured, women's garment manufacturers attracted between 4,000 and 5,000 buyers each year for the markets held in the city.[24]

In and around Dallas, manufacturers found an abundance of willing workers within commuting distance. Both Gartner and Zeman noted that the workers were not young, single women or young mothers with small children.[25] Instead the seamstresses were primarily middle-aged women who were looking for a way to enter the workforce and earn some extra cash.[26] Although the seamstresses were women, the cutters were always men, and in June of 1953, Cutters Local No. 387 of the International Ladies Garment Workers Union filed a complaint with the National Labor Relations Board against Page Boy. The complaint claimed that Page Boy management had interfered with attempts to unionize the workers and had refused to bargain with a legal union. Additionally, there were complaints because Abe Ravkind, Edna's husband, was listed as an employee of Page Boy—a problem for the unions since most regulations prevented owners and managers from also being workers. An investigation was held, and the preliminary finding exonerated Page Boy. In November the preliminary finding was upheld, and the NLRB stated that there was "no evidence of unfair labor practices" in the Page Boy plant.[27]

During the early years of the twentieth century, unionization in most states north of the Mason-Dixon line spread quickly. However, union organization in Texas was slow to develop, and conservative politics and the Texas right-to-work laws hindered unionization in Texas. In industrial states unions often signed agreements with manufacturers, making union membership mandatory for any person seeking employment with the company. These agreements forced workers to join unions prior to employment and forced workers to pay union dues. Often the dues were automatically withheld from the worker's paycheck by the company. The first union activity appeared in Dallas in 1934. In response to union drives, the manufacturers fired the union organizers. Then, in response to the firings, the union called a strike in 1935, but only about twenty percent of the Dallas garment workers participated in the strike. Just prior to World War II, Nardis Company and Sheba Ann Manufacturing, both Dallas manufacturers, signed contracts with the International Ladies Garment Workers Union—thus becoming the first Dallas manufacturing firms to unionize. The war slowed unionization, but as the war ended and manufacturers prospered, many garment manufacturers matched the wages and benefits being paid in union shops. These steps weakened the drive for unionization in Dallas, and the Texas union organizers turned their attention from Dallas to South Texas.

Texas politics also played a big part in the slow unionization of the area. Texas joined several other states by implementing right-to-work laws. These laws, supported under the Taft-Hartley Act, outlawed closed shops and prevented unions from making agreements with employers that required union membership in order to be hired. Not until the end of the century, when health care coverage and paid holidays became important issues with workers and unions began offering classes in English and other useful skills, did the unions regain some of their lost power in Dallas and across the state.[28]

With the labor problems settled the management of Page Boy felt secure about their future. Another design shift occurred in 1954. Although Page Boy continued to manufacture casual outfits, the company began to include more one-piece dresses, including an evening coat with fox trim around the cuffs that cost $69.95 and another coatdress with a large collar and bow for $39.95.

In one of Elsie's more candid interviews, she talked with Eleanor Roberts, a Boston-based journalist. The interview took place during the yearly Young Presidents' Organization advanced management seminar. Roberts described Elsie as the "petticoat president" and said that often the faculty at Harvard looked at Elsie with a puzzled expression, asking whether this really "was the president of Page Boy." The wide-ranging interview included information about the early models of the Page Boy maternity design. Elsie explained that she added "white touches" to most of the garments to brighten the styles up since many maternity dresses of the time were so drab and dull. She continued by saying that they had even tried an afternoon dress of crepe that had pleats, a fabric not typically used for maternity dresses. She described the first Page Boy workshop as a three-room attic over a cleaning and pressing business on Main Street. This article also included personal information, such as the names and ages of Edna's and Louise's children—information that Elsie rarely shared with the press. But the most personal information she gave about herself was her statement that she rarely worked after 5:30 p.m. unless it was absolutely necessary because she loved to go out dancing in one of the "dream dresses" that she had had custom made for her. Elsie said that she was "one of the few people" who could afford to purchase an $850 evening dress.[29]

The Page Boy seamstresses did all the sewing for the Page Boy fashions, but they also made many of the outfits that the sisters wore—especially Edna and Louise. And the sisters were not the only family members who benefited from having seamstresses at their beck and call. Edna and Louise's daughters benefited from the situation also. According to Joan Susman, Edna Frankfurt Ravkind's daughter, Page Boy workers made all the clothes she wore until she went away to college. Even as a young girl her clothes mirrored the outfits being produced in the Page Boy factory. In fact, the first day she attended seventh grade she wore a dress made in the factory. This dress was not only made from fabric that Page Boy included in the fall line, but it also had mink trim! And later, when her parents threw an ice-skating party for her birthday, the factory seamstresses designed a skating outfit from pink fabric lined in brown satin that was adorned with mink trim at the bottom of the skirt. If Page Boy used material or trim as a design element, the daughters often wore that

Newspaper advertisement of casual outfits showing bubble influence, early 1950s

same element on their clothes. Joan also recalled that she took dancing classes, and one year her mother volunteered to have the factory make all the costumes. One day shortly before the recital, Joan visited the factory. Instead of seeing maternity garments on the sewing machines, she saw all the seamstresses busily making cat costumes and filling the cats' tails with padding.[30]

Brenda Gartner Berg, Joan's cousin and Louise's daughter remembers that the factory also made many of the outfits that she wore. But even today she has mixed feelings about wearing those clothes. She remembers friends coming up and asking, "Did your mother make that?" Brenda was not sure whether the question was a compliment, meaning the garment was stylish, or whether it meant that the dress looked homemade.[31]

In 1955 *Good Housekeeping* magazine announced that it had selected a coordinated maternity wardrobe from the Page Boy line of clothing that it considered "the most exciting (wardrobe) of the season." The wardrobe consisted of five pieces. Page Boy shops in both Dallas and Los Angeles announced that they would give away one of the wardrobes to five women in each city.[32]

This type of publicity came easily to Page Boy and especially to Elsie, who by mid-decade was expanding her horizons. Elsie was again planning an extended tour of Europe to visit the couture fashion houses. As part of her trip, she arranged to send back fashion reports to the *Dallas Morning News*. Her first stop was in Ireland and England, where she reported on the use of woolens in London fashions. Her next stop was Rome. There she reported that she had bought twelve pairs of Italian heels and seen seven fashion shows. Many of the Italian designers were showing slim-line dresses and fur-trimmed costumes. Her next report began, "Paris at last." In contrast to Italy, the French were showing large coats with batwing sleeves. From Paris Elsie commented on the more outrageous styles, such as the dress made from Alcoa aluminum yarn. Finally, she reported that she liked Lanvin's collection with the high waistline, concluding that it "might very well influence my thinking in the next Page Boy silhouettes."[33]

In succeeding years Elsie continued attending regular Young Presidents' Organization annual management seminars at Harvard, and each time she attended, she herself became the center of attention. This attention was flattering but often also slightly demeaning. Eleanor Roberts, the women's editor of the *Boston Post* interviewed Elsie during several YPO seminar weeks. In 1956 she wrote a lengthy article about Elsie and her week at Harvard. She began by calling Elsie "elfin" and focused not only on the classes that Elsie was taking but on describing her clothes. Elsie said that for several years she had attended classes focused primarily on human relations and policy, but she was moving forward to management controls, which included budgets reports and delegating responsibility— something that Page Boy management had never learned. Elsie studied hard and took part in many of the late-night class discussions. She complained

about the schedule since she was not a morning person, saying that when at home she had breakfast in bed, but since she was forced to stay in a "suite at the Hotel Continental," she had to get up very early. Roberts also focused on Elsie's wardrobe, mentioning that she came to Boston with six suitcases filled "with gorgeous gowns by two of the country's top designers—Traina-Norell and Galanos." The "rest of her wardrobe" included a $12,000 mink coat, a beaver cape, ten pairs of shoes, and sixteen petticoats. When one of the other attendees mentioned that he wished that his wife dressed like Elsie did, Elsie refrained from telling him that she was wearing a $395 Galanos design.[34]

After Elsie's stay at Harvard in 1956, correspondent Marjorie Farnsworth described her as "a diminutive girl with an 18 inch waist." The columnist declared that Elsie had attended all the classes, including management, control, and budgeting. However, she also noted that Elsie's personal appearance was a surprise to the writer herself—as if a woman running a business should have appeared old and unattractive. Continuing her description of Elsie's life, Farnsworth declared that after each of the week-long seminars Elsie had returned to her rooms in the Pierre Hotel to recover from the intense studying and to check on the showroom activities. Although she could compete with men in business and management, her suite at the hotel could never be mistaken for that of a businessman. Farnsworth reported that Elsie's rooms were always filled with flowers and furs, including mink and chinchilla—a fur that Elsie had actually modeled for the chinchilla breeders association. She continued that Elsie left dresses thrown over much of the furniture in an attempt to separate the items that needed either to be cleaned or pressed from the fresh clothes. The one unqualified compliment that Farnsworth made was that after talking to her for a short time it became evident that Elsie had "a steel-trap mind."[35]

Later that year Page Boy opened another shop in California to serve Pasadena and the San Gabriel Valley. This brought the number of shops in the Los Angeles area to three. Other new locations included Detroit, Michigan, and Houston, Texas.[36]

During 1956 the styles were evolving again. Some of the sporty fashions remained, and many of these had slim shorts and leg-hugging toreador pants. These might be paired with long tops. Page Boy was manufacturing the pants of clinging heavy cotton knit that did not sag.[37] But many of the previous styles were being replaced. Instead of the sporty denim and polished-cotton separates, Page Boy featured dresses with empire waistlines that reflected Elsie's recent trip to Europe. Many of the column dresses were accompanied by bolero jackets. Some Page Boy dresses had buttons down the front, which concealed an inset release pleat. As the wearer unbuttoned the buttons, the pleats opened, providing extra room for the mother-to-be. Dresses were made in rich fabrics, and as before Page Boy specialized in high-fashion details. According to Elsie, "You can't hide the fact that you're expecting a child . . . but you can detract from it."[38]

Elsie began 1957 as usual by attending the Har-

vard seminars, but just prior to going to Boston, she made a stop in Washington, D.C., to attend the inauguration and the inaugural ball for the second Eisenhower term. While in Washington she was interviewed for the papers. During the interview she declared that the one-piece empire-waist dress that diverted attention away from the natural waist actually helped the mother-to-be psychologically because the slim line of the style mimicked the very slender tight-fitting dresses that were fashionable during that season.[39]

Elsie was interviewed about her attendance at the Harvard seminars, and she mentioned that her attendance was easier as the years went by since by the end of the decade a few other women had become members of the YPO. She recalled that at the second or third meeting she attended, the men had all stayed on campus in dorms. But since Harvard was an all-male school, there was no place for her to stay. She was forced to stay in a hotel in the central part of Boston about thirty minutes by cab from the seminars. She felt that this was an imposition for her since the men could walk to the classrooms in just minutes whereas she was forced to get up earlier to get breakfast and travel to the classes. Furthermore, she was forced to travel back to her hotel in the evening and thus often missed some of the nightly study sessions. She also told the reporter that after each grueling week she treated herself to a memento—a gold charm that she attached to a gold bracelet.[40]

Throughout the next few years Page Boy continued to focus on dresses. These silhouettes reflected Elsie's thoughts as she expressed them in her column dated August 7, 1956. Again she emphasized that she used the Paris fashion shows as inspiration for the Page Boy designs. In February of 1957, Page Boy featured a French schoolgirl look with an empire jumper dress and white blouse. Page Boy was also pairing with fabric manufacturers and promoting specialty fabrics. In one outfit the dress was made of textured cotton by Fuller and the white blouse by Wamsutta textiles. The caption noted that the entire outfit was washable—something that would be important to housewives but not particularly important to working women, who might send their clothes to the cleaners.[41]

The end of the midcentury decade was marked by changing attitudes and styles, and different women began to influence fashion. Whereas in the 1930s and 1940s movie stars often hid the fact that they were pregnant, in the 1950s Hollywood played up the family life of the stars. Magazine articles focused on Hollywood couples and even featured their homes and children. Many young stars began to be seen while pregnant and even appeared in advertisements wearing Page Boy designs that reflected these new ideas. Some of the new designs focused on two-piece sports outfits with plaids and print tops and leggings for bottoms. In November of 1957, Page Boy publicized a list of new television and movie stars who were wearing its clothing. According to Gay Simpson, the *Dallas Morning News* fashion editor, Helen O'Connell from Dave Garroway's program was introducing Page Boy fashions.[42] "Debbie Reynolds, who also proudly answers to the name of Mrs. Eddie Fisher, has just bought a Page Boy wardrobe. The Princess of Monaco [Grace Kelly], (mother of Princess Caroline), maintained her best-dressed status in her Page Boy clothes, as did Mrs. Mike Todd [Elizabeth Taylor], who was seen in a newspaper photograph wearing the latest Page Boy fashion."

The wide range of styles and fabrics offered in the Page Boy line increased the appeal of Page Boy fashions to the stars. A celebrity could find a casual outfit trimmed in knit fabric or a blue taffeta evening dress. Moreover Page Boy styles were still fashioned so that the dresses could look sleek and slim during the early months of pregnancy and then, according to the wearer's changing body, change some parts of the style such as unbuttoning the buttons running down the front to allow more room in the width of the dress for the later months of the pregnancy.[43]

Elsie ended 1957 by receiving another award. This one came from the Business and Professional Women's Club of Dallas, which was honoring ten Dallas women for their accomplishments in the world of both business and professions.[44] But the year also brought style changes that hit the maternity business hard because many regular ready-to-wear styles could be worn as maternity dresses. In fact, *Houston Post* columnist Virginia McCallon wrote, "Last spring was the luckiest season of all for expectant mothers. Chemise and Trapeze silhouettes made maternity dresses look like all the other newest styles. Figures were easily camouflaged. . . . This spring there are still some styles that bypass the waistline" such as Empire influences, middies and tunics.[45] As with other manufacturers Page Boy was simultaneously fighting and embracing the revolution in fashion called the "chemise" or "sack dress."

In an attempt to overcome the new problems caused by the current styles, Elsie began traveling even more than she had in previous years. Thus, in January she traveled to Washington, D.C., to show off the new line of dresses at several Julius Garfinckle & Co. locations. While in Washington she was interviewed by Ruth Wagner, a columnist for the *Washington Post*. Elsie said that the sack dresses would be "wonderful for the woman who's expecting." However, she also gave a warning to mothers-to-be who might be tempted to buy regular ready-to-wear rather than maternity fashions for their wardrobe. She noted that most of the regular-size dresses were cut too slim from the waist down because, although they were not fitted at the waist, the skirts were intended to fit snuggly just below the waist, and the styles were tapered from the hipline to the hem. She pointed out that some of these dresses looked better when they were worn with a girdle that not only cinched in the hips but also flattened the "derriere." Elsie said that, although Page Boy was making dresses that looked like the chemise, pattern cutting was tricky and the dresses needed to be cut "just right" so that they would fit a pregnant body.[46] Additionally she said that each design needed to be cut on a maternity block to insure proper fit. Conceding that she did not

own a chemise because she herself preferred the tightly belted dresses that showed off her eighteen-inch waist, she predicted that fully fifty percent of the maternity clothing manufactured for 1959 would include one-piece chemise dresses. Interestingly, during this interview Elsie stated that she was the head designer, although a few months earlier in an interview for the *Dallas Times Herald*, Elsie had said that Louise was the "sole designer for the firm."[47]

Neither of these statements was exactly accurate since over the years Page Boy had employed and continued to employ other designers. In fact, in 1956 two of their designers had won recognition for their designs for the Dallas Little Theater production of *Strange Bedfellows*. The designers, Wayne Steele and Harry Hoppenjans, Jr., designed for the stage as a sideline, while designing "commercially for Page Boy Maternity Manufacturing Company."[48]

During the latter part of the 1950s, Page Boy increased the amount of new, man-made fabrics it was using in the design and manufacture of its styles. After the war the company had always focused on high-end fashions made from natural fabrics such as silk, woolens, linen, or polished cotton, which lost its sheen if it was washed. All these fabrics needed to be dry-cleaned or laundered and ironed. Now some of their styles were made in easy-care drip-dry or wash-and-wear fabrics.[49] Page Boy's advertisements had never focused on the ease of the care of the garments since many ads were aimed at high-end shoppers; however, since the print description of the new fabrics focused on the ease of care, clearly the com-

Elsie in her favorite Norell suit with
Florence Henderson, ca. 1957

styles, including a bubble dress and tightly fitting tapered pants, Elsie noted that she made yearly trips to Europe, that she was aware of "Givenchy's shift to the chemise," and that Page Boy was adapting the new Chanel suits for maternity wear.[50]

Both Edna and Elsie wore designer clothing. However, not all the haute couture garments they bought were added to their wardrobes. Instead, these garments were delivered to the Page Boy factory where the sisters practiced a little business espionage. There they disassembled the garments into their component parts to see how they were constructed and how the pieces fit together. Then they worked out the designs to see how they could convert them into maternity garments. So, true to their claim, they did not create designs, but they did interpret them—perhaps more closely than the original designers knew.[51]

Elsie traveled all around the country, speaking at shop openings and giving interviews about maternity fashions. During one of her trips to Washington, D.C., Elsie met with Jayne Meadows, who was pictured with Elsie and was wearing a Page Boy outfit for the photo shoot. The photograph of Jayne Meadows and Elsie Frankfurt also appeared in such weekly magazines as *All Florida Magazine*. Meadows also served as moderator for a Page Boy style show while wearing one of her Page Boy designs. During the interview for this photo shoot, Elsie offered her own thoughts about various aspects of women's fashion. She said that she preferred capes over coats because they could make a "statement" and continued that capes had become her own distinctive fash-

pany wanted to highlight that point. Moreover, these fabrics made the designs more accessible to busy mothers-to-be on a budget. Even while making dresses more accessible to a wider audience, Page Boy also wanted customers to know that the company still focused on high-style designs. In one full-page spread that highlighted some of the newer

PAGE BOY

*fashion
magazine
for
smart
young
mothers-
to-be*

COVER FASHION DETAILS:
PLEASE TURN PAGE

**FALL
AND
WINTER
1952**

have a pretty **P**regnancy...

Page Boy

New interest, new texture suit of Bengaline rayon cuffs. Rhinestone buttons adjustment skirt. Blue

in Page Boy's profile-pretty faille with metallic knit collar, add a share of sparkle. Cut-out lagoon, metal, copper. Sizes 10-18. Style 855. 39.95

Front cover of Page Boy fall/winter catalog, 1952.

Back cover of Page Boy fall/winter catalog, 1952.

Front and back of Jackie Kennedy dress,
courtesy of University of North Texas.

Front cover of Page Boy fall/holiday
1978 collection.

Black velvet paisley border top with winter
white worsted pants, and primrose tent
dress with full cuffed sleeves. Featured in
the Fall/Holiday 1978 collection.

Black knit body suit under a plaid evening jumper, and matching pantsuit.
Featured in the Fall/Holiday 1978 collection.

Top left: Organza dress highlighted by black sequins. Featured in 1983 fall/holiday catalog.

Top right: Flowing blue and black dress. Featured in 1983 fall/holiday catalog.

Bottom left: Accordion-pleated tunic over a double-layered skirt. Featured in 1984 fall/holiday catalog.

Bottom right: Red knit dress with black and royal appliqués. Featured in 1984 fall/holiday catalog.

Right: Magenta wool blend suit with soft pink blouse. Featured in fall/holiday 1986 catalog.

Left: Black velvet one-piece blouson with jet buttons. Featured in fall/holiday 1986 catalog.

Left: Striped and dotted blouson with pleated skirt, and jacket with crepe blouse with straight skirt. Featured in 1987 spring/summer catalog.

Right: Rayon faille dress tucked across the back. Featured in 1987 spring/summer catalog.

Dress Finesse. This retrospective rayon faille dress is tucked across the back for a soft flowing fit. Sizes 4-16. $125.00 (Style 1286). Mid-February delivery.

Watercolor Florals. Mix these tissue faille separates for that special weekend, or wear them to the office. Our soft jacket is perfect over our white lined shell and easy fitting pant. Sizes PSML. Jacket $79.00 (Style 3390). Shell, also available in floral, $45.00 (Style 3392). Pant, $49.00 (Style 5552).

Our versatile cardigan style blouson works well with the knife-pleated skirt or floral pant. Sizes PSML. Blouson, $69.00 (Style 3388). Skirt, also available in solid white, $59.00 (Style 4030).

Left: Rosette tunic with slim skirt in wool
blend jersey. Featured in 1988 fall catalog.

Right: Black velvet and lace over a fuchsia taffeta shirt with
back bow. Featured in 1988 fall catalog.

Black cotton sweater with bright border with mock turtleneck and fuchsia corduroy skirt, and purple cotton sweater with corduroy pants in purple. Featured in 1988 fall catalog.

Silk jacquard dress with batwing sleeve. Featured in 1988 spring/ summer catalog.

Silk jacquard dress with asymmetrical double skirt. Featured in 1988 spring/ summer catalog.

Crinkled faille trapeze top over slim skirt. Featured in 1988 spring/summer catalog.

Purle cotton jersey tunic with orange leggings, and purple cotton jersey jump-suit with green turtleneck. Featured in 1989 fall/holiday catalog.

Burgundy checked suit in rayon.
Featured in 1989 fall/holiday catalog.

Eggplant two-piece dress with passementerie embroidery, and bow back dress. Featured in 1989 fall/holiday catalog.

Toffee rayon suit, and jumper in wine with embroidered white blouse. Featured in 1989 fall/holiday catalog.

Black velvet and satin dress with bow-trimmed back. Featured in 1989 fall/holiday catalog.

Black and white blouson with bow-trimmed back.
Featured in 1989 spring/summer catalog.

Rayon/silk fuchsia suit and white blouse with embroidery. Featured in 1989 spring/summer catalog.

Turquoise sundress, and periwinkle tee shirt banded in turquoise with periwinkle pants. Featured in 1989 spring/summer catalog.

Fuchsia/tangerine tunic, and turquoise cardigan and yellow button front top with turquoise pants. Featured in 1989 spring/summer catalog.

Left: Hand-beaded tunic over sequinned skirt. Featured in 1990 spring catalog.

Above right: Hip-wrap top with coordinating shorts. Featured in 1990 spring/ summer catalog.

Bottom right: Javanese-inspired jumpsuit, and navy and white cotton sun-dress. Featured in 1990 spring/summer catalog.

From left to right: black cotton catsuit with zipper-front mock turtle; black, gold, and fuchsia plaid suit; hand-beaded crepe chemise; and daisy-print brocade cocktail dress. All featured in the 1991 fall catalog.

As featured editorially
in the May 1959 issue of
GLAMOUR MAGAZINE . . . these
exciting, made-for-the-
season PAGE BOYS. Come
in to your nearest PAGE BOY
MATERNITY SHOP and ask to
see them all.

1959 mockup of Page Boy advertisement in *Glamour*

ion symbol. Furthermore, illustrating that Elsie was not just a businesswoman but a style setter herself, she admitted that her own favorite designers were James Galanos and Norman Norell.[52]

Always available to offer her own ideas and to promote Page Boy styles, Elsie told fashion columnist Berta Mohr that she felt that a pregnant woman's clothes should "be geared to her type, just as her other clothes are." A woman should not be required to change her personality or life style while pregnant. She continued that Page Boy keyed its designs to individual style preferences and to "prevailing fashion." Many of the garments could pass as regular ready-to-wear and be worn after delivery.[53] This idea that women should not hide their pregnancy and should be able to find clothes that suited their lifestyle and fashion sense was one of the major ideas that Elsie and Page Boy styles promoted. The illustration that accompanied the article depicted a slim-line jumper with an inverted center pleat that could be buttoned closed during early pregnancy and then opened to create more room later in the pregnancy and perhaps even closed again and worn after delivery.

Later that year Elsie was off on another trip—this time to study Hawaiian fashions. And like any good business manager, the trip combined a holiday and a Young Presidents' Organization meeting with her desire to study the flowing lines of island dress. After analyzing the island styles, Elsie decided that muumuus could be adapted for maternity dresses just as the trapeze dress had been adapted to conceal the pregnancy.[54]

A few months later Elsie was in California because Page Boy was opening a new Wilshire Boulevard shop. The new store contained a specialty department called "Casual Corner" that carried clothing created especially for the Californian outdoor lifestyle. The clothes carried in the Casual Corner focused on cool playclothes, such as a bubble swimsuit with built-in bra and shorts that sported expansion buttons at the waist band. Manufactured in brightly colored fabrics, the clothes offered in the Casual Corner included shorts, pedal pushers, Capri pants, and bathing suits, all sports outfits that fit the California way of life. Each of the outfits also had coordinated cover-up tops. Additionally, the Casual Corner area of the store contained its own fitting rooms so that the store maintained a division of styles. Cocktail dresses, evening outfits, and more formal business clothes were shown in the main section of the store. At the opening, the shop served pickles and strawberries, catering to the supposed whims of the pregnant customers. Elsie moderated a fashion show and highlighted the new styles, including chemise, trapeze, and bubble dresses.

Elsie also brought the maternity fashion dolls to California so that they could be on display for the store opening.[55] By this time the dolls were nearly ten years old and beginning to show some wear and tear from all the travel. The next month Elsie returned to California to help celebrate the second anniversary of the opening of the Pasadena store, and during the following month she was appointed to be chairman of the "Maternity Dress Industry for the United States Committee for the United Nations." Elsie, the inveterate jet setter, willingly accepted this position, which required travel and would also bring public recognition to Page Boy.[56]

Within six months Page Boy had divided the two sections of the Wilshire Boulevard maternity shops housing the Casual Corner and opened a second store called Casual Corner.[57] This new store, located one block from the original location with about 2,000 square feet of floor space, catered to "casual year-round California living." Instead of the clothes being lined up on the sides of the store, as had been usual, the clothes were displayed in a central round fixture decorated in a "circus motif." This shop also housed a "craving corner," which continued to offer pickles, strawberries, and Chinese fortune cookies containing paper predictions of "boy" or "girl."[58]

By the close of the decade, Page Boy had opened ten stand-alone shops that it controlled. Three were located in Dallas. One was located in the headquarters building on Cedar Springs, one on South Ervay, and one on Berkshire near the corner of Preston Road and North West Highway. The company had another shop in Houston near what is now Rice Village on Rice Boulevard. There were three shops in the Los Angeles area, two on Wilshire Boulevard, with one located in Beverly Hills, and one in Los Angeles proper, and one in Pasadena. The other three shops were located in the Midwest, one in Cleveland and two in Detroit.

Chapter 4

Jackie, Yoga, and Novel Advertising

By the beginning of the 1960s, Page Boy had experienced twenty years of phenomenal success. Although Elsie never publicly revealed how old she was, she turned fifty in 1961, and Edna had already turned fifty in 1958. The baby of the family, Louise, turned forty in 1962. As the sisters passed these milestones, the business faced new challenges, making change inevitable. During the past decade Page Boy had prospered even as the baby boom slowed. More critically, the sisters faced continual business challenges.

Edna, who had not had a specific job description, although she managed the manufacturing arm of the business, realized that she needed a personal outlet from the stress and tension of long work hours. She developed an interest in ballroom dancing, and she and her husband took dancing lessons. Within a short time they began to compete, and they

Button-front skimmer
dress, ca. 1960

became world-class competitive ballroom dancers.[1] Louise had a third child, and although she still worked in the business, her family beckoned. Elsie, ever competitive, looked for greater challenges. Even with these increasing activities the women focused on growing the firm, and they continued to closely watch the fashion trendsetters.

After John Kennedy won the presidential election in 1960, his young wife became a sophisticated fashion icon. Jackie Kennedy exuded style, and since she was pregnant when Kennedy was nominated, her influence was felt in the field of maternity fashions as well as regular ready-to-wear. Jackie began creating her own style sense in the late 1950s, and by the time her husband was elected, her style had become a model of what all young women wanted to wear. In previous decades maternity styles had ranged from two-piece fitted skirts sporting the cut-out window or stretch pants with tunic tops to the chemise and bubble dress. As Mrs. Kennedy's styles grew into the fashion standard, it became apparent that she preferred simplified one-piece dresses for all occasions. Many of her outfits were cut with a slim or princess silhouette, and she continued to wear similar styles throughout her pregnancies. Suddenly a fashion leader was often seen in maternity clothes, and many of the five million pregnant women clamored to emulate her style. When asked about Kennedy's fashion tastes, Elsie Frankfurt noted that Page Boy was manufacturing coat dresses and short, slim dresses that reflected the Kennedy fashion choices. Although Elsie never revealed di-

rectly whether or not any of the Kennedy women were wearing Page Boy designs, she did indicate that Ethel Kennedy, Jackie's sister-in-law, "was an indirect customer" of Page Boy since she and all of the Kennedy women were shopping in Washington where Page Boy designs were readily available.[2]

Jacqueline Kennedy became the only celebrity whom Elsie never used for publicity, never naming her as a customer. The Kennedy name never appeared in any of the lists of Page Boy clients that Elsie recited, and she never claimed a Kennedy as a direct patron. But Mrs. Kennedy had been a client of Page Boy at least before her husband was elected president. The three sisters must have decided to keep this a secret but also to save the information for posterity. On March 9, 1961, less than two months after John F. Kennedy was inaugurated, Page Boy donated one royal-blue wool dress to the Museum of Fashion, Dallas Fashion Arts. The donation record indicated that the dress was "worn by Mrs. John. F. Kennedy prior to the birth of her second child while Senator Kennedy was running for the presidency of the United States and while he was President-elect." Furthermore, the acquisition data indicated that Mrs. Kennedy purchased the dress at Lord & Taylor in New York and that she had been "photographed in the dress many times." According to the acquisition date she even wore the dress when she was interviewed by Dave Garroway on the *Today* show.[3] However, the actual provenance of this garment is in question. Although the acquisition data sheet says that "this dress was worn by Mrs. John F. Kennedy"

Front view of wool dress worn by
Jacqueline Kennedy, 1960

Back view of dress worn by Jacqueline
Kennedy, 1960

Jackie, Yoga, and Novel Advertising

and even provides the name of the store where it was purchased—which matches the label on the dress—Myra Walker, director of the Texas Fashion Collection at Denton, Texas, where the dress is preserved, questions whether this is the actual dress that Kennedy wore.

Three years later Kennedy was pregnant again, and columnists asked rhetorical questions about what she planned to wear. Newspapers included columns such as "We Await Mrs. Kennedy's Style Cue" and "The Jackie Influence: Get Ready for Another Trend." In answer to questions about whether Kennedy had purchased a new wardrobe, Gay Paulet announced that Mrs. Kennedy would "make do" with dresses and maternity clothes she already had in her closet. "For no matter what Mrs. Kennedy wears, she is copied—in hair style, in the slim-cut sleeveless dress, in the mantilla head covering. . . . She already has purchased several dresses that are slim through the bodice but flaring toward the hemline." Page Boy marketed the same styles, and Elsie observed that women came into the shops and commented, "This is the same silhouette Mrs. Kennedy is wearing."[4]

Even though Paulet said that Jacqueline Kennedy would make do with what she already had, many designers tried to get their names in the paper in association with the news of Mrs. Kennedy's pregnancy. Elsie Frankfurt told columnist Anne Yates Clarke that the Kennedy influence had changed the styles and that now over sixty percent of the outfits sold were one-piece dresses rather than two-piece outfits. She said they did not know whether Mrs.

Kennedy was going to wear their clothes but they were "enthusiastic about the fact that Mrs. Robert Kennedy had recently bought three new Page Boy dresses." Although Oleg Cassini was unavailable for comment, one of his staff was willing to comment and said that "it would be a few weeks" before they would answer any questions. Designers Nancy Herlinger for Nan Dee and Howard Oxenberg for Helene Scott Maternities gave vague answers when asked about Mrs. Kennedy's clothes.[5]

About this time Page Boy began what was to become a long relationship with another public figure, Florence Henderson. Elsie as usual was in New York during the winter, and in February she was showing the latest Page Boy styles. The *Today* show producers invited her to present part of the line to Dave Garroway and his audience. Elsie brought the clothes to the television studio where she met Ms. Henderson—the "*Today* Girl." At the beginning of the style show, she introduced Ms. Henderson to the audience, remarking that Henderson was wearing a Page Boy fashion in green crepe. Elsie then turned the microphone over to Ms. Henderson, who gave the commentary for the style show.[6] It is not clear how often Elsie appeared on the *Today* show. In 1957 she appeared as a fashion expert, and several years later she appeared again, displaying both the maternity dolls and also presenting Page Boy maternity fashions.[7] Soon, Elsie herself became a regular on television, and in 1963 she even appeared on *To Tell the Truth*.[8]

The next summer Henderson was interviewed

while she was playing summer stock in the San Francisco area. Henderson's children were accompanying her on her trip and were with her during the interview, so the conversation evolved to a discussion about working and having children. She explained that she had been pregnant the previous year while she was a "regular" on the Dave Garroway show. She continued, "I kept working until I was eight months pregnant, . . . and every day at the end of the show, the announcer's voice would come on saying, 'Miss Henderson's maternity clothes courtesy of Page Boy.'"[9] This type of voice-over was a common occurrence in the 1950s and 1960s and allowed a company to get television publicity. The only cost to the company was the cost of the clothes worn by the actor or actress.

Thee years later Elsie approached Florence Henderson again. Page Boy was planning a style show in the Cotillion Room at the Pierre Hotel in New York, and Elsie wanted Henderson to provide the commentary for the show. This show, planned for July, would display the fall styles to nearly 250 invited fashion writers. Henderson said she would love to do the announcing, but she herself was in the ninth month of her pregnancy—for the third time. Elsie assured her that there would be no problem, and for this occasion Elsie fitted her with a crepe empire-waist dress in red. The July style show introduced several new fashion ideas, including a royal blue tunic top with slit sides and frogs sewn above the side slits.[10] The pants were created with the new stretchable Helanca panel under the tunic, rather than the usual Page Boy cut-out.[11] Many of the design ideas included in this show were created by model Ruth Newmann, who had collaborated with Page Boy and wanted the garments to be free flowing and unrestricted. Newmann modeled several outfits in the style show and delivered a baby the next day. Other styles included a long, sheer wool formal dress with a tie just under the bust-line. The ties, which were sewn into the side seams, allowed the dress to fit under the bust and flow freely in the back. Additional designs included jumpers, blouses, and long dresses. The photographer took pictures of the models, but he also took pictures of Henderson wearing several Page Boy outfits. One was a fake fur jumper.[12] Along with Henderson and Newmann, all the other models in the show were also pregnant. At the end of the show, Henderson quipped, "All these women are going to have babies—I hope they have husbands too!"[13]

The year 1963 became the year of tent dresses and shifts, and depending on exactly how the dresses were cut, many of them could be worn by any woman—pregnant or not. Even fashion writers noted that many of the most fashionable everyday styles could also be worn as maternity dresses. Although the styles were innovative, the shape of these styles hurt the sales of maternity clothes. For example, the maternity shop styles in the the New York Department store Bonwit Teller "echoed" styles found elsewhere in the store. These fashions severed the important barrier that had previously existed between maternity clothes and regular ready-to-wear. Chicago

Moygashel linen and lace skirt and top, 1950s

fashion editor Frances Borzello reported that, in addition to finding dresses in the ready-to-wear section, "ladies-in-waiting were finding dresses among the beach shifts and smocks found in the sportswear department."[14]

Facing this new challenge, both Elsie and Edna realized the increased importance of "star power." Elsie convinced movie stars to pose for advertisements, and Edna knew how to sell to them. Teen idol Bobby Darin and his wife Sandra Dee visited Dallas twice in the late summer and fall of 1961. Dee was pregnant, and Darin, wanting only the best for his wife, made an appointment at Page Boy. He told Edna he wanted something fabulous for his wife. Edna knew that she had several outfits that would be perfect for Dee. The couple arrived for their appointment, and Edna personally waited on them. Darin made his decision—selecting the "fabulous" outfit and said he wanted to buy it. Edna, without taking a breath or hesitating, raised the price because she knew that Darin would think it was more "fabulous" if the garment had a higher price.[15]

Since the usual Page Boy skirt with the cut-out in the middle did not lend itself to the sleek lines and skirts with short tops that were the current fashion, Elsie announced that "the cut-out skirt is dead," and Jackie's classic dresses, dresses with clean lines, became a standard for the 1960s. To fight the slump in sales and still cling to her own fashion ideas, Elsie announced that Page Boy had a new invention: "The Skirt." According to Elsie, the new design had no buttons, no hooks, no zippers, no drawstrings, and definitely no cut-outs. The new style had a stretchy waistband and two inset panels at the sides. As the figure expanded, gathered panels along the side of the skirt would widen to allow the skirt to accommodate a larger waistline. Pockets were designed on each side of the skirt so they could camouflage the panels.[16] The panels were made of Helanca.[17] Most importantly, with the stretch fabric inset, the skirt could maintain the tapered silhouette and still allow a slim hemline. With this new style, the overblouses or tops could be cut much shorter, reaching to about the hip bone, because the skirt fabric extended higher toward the waist.

With great fanfare Page Boy announced the "invention" of this new skirt, and the news was carried in the fashion section of papers across the nation, including the *Christian Science Monitor*. Monitor columnist "Aline"[18] reported on the new skirt in her column "Through Texas Eyes." The article quoted Elsie, stating that Page Boy's new designs were "as simple as Mrs. John Kennedy's"; furthermore, Elsie claimed that the skirt design had been submitted for a patent and was patent pending number 174055.[19] Elsie also declared that, because of the new inset design, the garments with the new system could be worn as maternity clothes and could also be worn as street clothes after the baby was born. The stretchy waistband would allow the band to extend as the abdomen enlarged and then later return to the prepregnancy size.[20] A careful search of patents granted around that time indicates, however, that the patent was never issued. Many outfits included in this line

also had double seams in both the blouses and skirts so that the garments could be let out to fit the fuller figure of the pregnant woman and later be taken up if the wearer wanted to use the outfit as regular clothing. Jane Guzman, a historian and family friend of the Frankfurts, said that this innovation allowed women to look well groomed throughout their pregnancy because the garments fit snugly early in their pregnancies and then accommodated the fuller pregnant figure later in their pregnancies.[21] Both Guzman and her mother had worn Page Boy maternity clothes, and they both knew the sisters and their children.

In early fall of 1963, Elsie was interviewed for the financial news section of the *San Diego Union*. The wide-ranging article covered Page Boy's history and described in length the opening of the new Page Boy outlet in San Diego. Elsie declared that Page Boy could dress women looking for high fashion in all price ranges. She mentioned that they had slacks for as little as $9.98 and sold dresses for over $250. But in this article she also made a statement that she rarely did—she complimented her sister Louise and credited her with much of the Page Boy success because Louise had the "ability to follow and interpret style trends from Paris and elsewhere, leading to an average of five new lines of maternity wear each year." She continued that, because of Page Boy's strong financial position, the sisters did not need to justify any of their decisions to bankers or anyone else. Finally, Elsie stated that she was the president, but she characterized both of her sisters as vice pres-

Double-seam of skirt, allowing room for skirt to
be let out several inches, late 1950s

idents, an unusual statement that was not repeated.[22]

Elsie had always sought public attention for
Page Boy and never allowed any instance to pass
without the viewers or readers knowing when a celebrity wore a Page Boy outfit. Nevertheless, public
knowledge and beliefs about maternity clothes and
pregnant women often did not correspond with actual facts. For example, about twenty years after Elsie
and Page Boy had forged a relationship with the *Today* show and Florence Henderson, Jane Pauley announced that she was leaving the United States to
report on the wedding of Sarah Ferguson to Prince
Andrew and that when she returned she would take
an eleven-week maternity leave from the *Today* show.

After this announcement she gave an interview
about her experience in television, in which she
commented on how things in the broadcast industry
had changed for women, and especially for women
who were pregnant. "In 1960 when Florence Henderson was on *Today*, NBC hid her pregnancy behind clotheslines and parasols and wouldn't let her
mention it on the air." Pauley, in contrast had spoken
about her own pregnancy on the air and also noted
that she had not missed any work.[23] Evidently Pauley
had been told or believed that Henderson's pregnancy had been hidden from the audience, but when
one reads what Henderson herself said in 1961, it is
evident that the audience and viewers must have
been aware that Henderson was pregnant because
each day as the *Today* show ended the show announcer attributed Ms. Henderson's maternity
wardrobe to Page Boy. Moreover since Page Boy only
made maternity clothes, it had to be clear that she
was pregnant—why else would she be wearing maternity clothes? Also, since Elsie commented about
the Page Boy dress that Henderson wore during the
style show, it had to be obvious that she was pregnant. Perhaps Henderson never overtly discussed
her condition on air as Pauley did, but according to
her own statements, it was not hidden, and Henderson's position on the *Today* show was significantly
different from that of Pauley.

Managing Page Boy and promoting its merchandise kept the sisters busy every day and all year.
Nevertheless, each sister discovered that it was important to bring other dimensions to their lives. Al-

though the older sisters found outlets in their own pursuits—ballroom dancing for Edna and travel for Elsie—Louise looked within and began studying yoga. She also became interested in eating health foods and studying alternative diets to alleviate the stress of raising a family and working full-time. During this time Louise introduced her sisters to her new-found stress reliever and encouraged them to join her as she did her yoga exercises.[24]

In 1962 the sisters took a vacation together, and they rented a bungalow at Rancho La Puerta in Tecate, Mexico, just south of the California border. After they arrived in Mexico, they discovered that Indra Devi, the leading yoga advocate in the Western hemisphere, was offering classes at her nearby yoga institute in Tecate. Since the sisters had come to relax and were already interested in yoga, they joined the classes.[25]

Before meeting the Frankfurt sisters in Mexico, Ms. Devi had traveled around the United States promoting a program she called "Yoga for Americans." She believed that the American lifestyle was filled with stress, and she felt that Americans needed to learn how to relax. During her travels she offered demonstrations and actively sought a factory or workplace where she might introduce a yoga break into the workday. Even after offering free lessons, Devi was unable to find any factory owner or manager willing to launch her program. This chance meeting with Louise, Edna, and Elsie brought the innovative Page Boy owners and the eager yoga instructor together.

Thrilled by the revitalization and relaxation they gained by participating in Devi's regimen, the Frankfurt sisters decided to bring Devi to Dallas so she could introduce her plan in the Page Boy factory. In commenting about this trip, Elsie said that the sisters "felt better. They worked better. They snoozed fine . . . [and] even their figures were trimmer."[26]

The sisters returned to Dallas and outfitted all the employees from secretaries to janitors with their own yoga mats. They followed through with their plan by bringing Ms. Devi to Dallas to teach classes at the Page Boy factory. Madame Devi observed all the workers and created specific exercises for each division of the company. The workers were able to remain in their own working area to do the exercises. Each session began with synchronized breathing and stretches. This was followed by relaxation exercises, and the session ended with a general meditative period. Secretaries practiced relaxing their eyes and learned how to use their typewriters to support their elbows while holding their heads in their hands. Shipping clerks, who worked standing on their feet all day, were instructed in how to relieve the tension in their feet by doing a reverse posture. In this position the worker lay on the floor with her legs raised parallel to the tables. The knees were bent over the tops of the tables, elevating the body from their heels while the shoulders rested on the ground. This position flexed the legs at the knees and hips and stretched the back without putting any weight on the feet. Cutters and the women who worked with them stretched out on cutting tables, and others stretched out on the floor. Elsie and Louise served as models and demonstrated some of the positions and exercise techniques.[27]

After Ms. Devi's visit the sisters wove the yoga break into the factory's daily routine. Each day the Page Boy plant closed down promptly at 2 p.m. The switchboard operators interrupted all calls at 1:55 with the announcement that "yoga break starts at 2! And the switchboard will be turned off."[28] The janitor participated by lying down near the broom closet, as did the comptroller, John H. Fulda, who practiced at his desk. Even William J. Moser, the sales manager, participated in the show room.[29] Retail customers and buyers from department stores who were visiting the Page Boy showroom to place an order were told that business would stop; they could either wait until the session was over or they could join in. One of the sisters conducted the exercise regimen by calling it out over the loudspeaker system, or if the sisters were not available, an employee played a recording of the exercises. The yoga break did not replace the regular three o'clock work break but instead supplemented it. This kept the employees happy. Ever the mathematician with a sharpened pencil, Elsie asserted that the break cost the company $10,530 each year in work lost by the 150 employees. Nevertheless, she believed that the break contributed much more than it cost because it increased efficiency and raised employee morale.[30]

In November Kermit Jaediker, a writer for the *New York Daily News,* picked up the yoga story and wrote a two-part article focusing on Elsie Frankfurt and Page Boy's yoga break. In the first installment he explained that Elsie wanted to "stand everyone in the U.S. on his or her head, literally." The article pointed out that Elsie shunned the more mystical side of yoga in favor of meditation and exercise to relieve tension. When Jaediker visited Elsie in her hotel suite, she demonstrated her exercise routine. She also mentioned that she planned to encourage the buyers at Page Boy's New York showroom to try yoga. Jaediker added that information about yoga had been placed in the library at the Page Boy retail outlet in the main building. Customers shopping in the factory store had access to the library.[31]

Never shy about taking advantage of any opportunity for free advertising, Elsie had the yoga exercises photographed by well-known photographer Shel Hershorn so they could be used in a photo spread that appeared in the February 14, 1964, issue of *Life.* The article "*Life* Goes to a Yoga (Not a Coffee) Break: Heels over Heads for Efficiency" contained several of Hershorn's photographs. All three sisters appeared in one photograph, and in another picture the porter, Jimmy Shoemake, was even photographed lying on his back. His cap was neatly placed in the middle of that photograph facing the camera. The cap had the words "Page Boy Co." clearly stitched on the front. So, even in an article about the company's yoga break, Elsie got the Page Boy name in the middle of one picture.[32]

Arlene Dahl, an actress and beauty consultant, picked up the yoga story in her syndicated column about health and beauty titled "Let's Be Beautiful."

Dahl described the yoga break as a beauty aid and suggested that workers should be given "beauty breaks" when they could opt to do deep breathing and stretching exercises for five or ten minutes each day. Dahl admonished employers for not picking up the idea, and she suggested that the workers try the system for themselves. Often when Elsie gave interviews about yoga, she mentioned that she had been on tranquilizers prior to learning yoga and beginning a meditation regimen. Then she would comment that after she learned how to carry out yoga exercises, she no longer needed the tranquilizers. In fact, she thought yoga was better than tranquilizers, and thus she wanted to share this benefit with her employees.[33]

Elsie took credit for almost all of the Page Boy accomplishments. For example, in the majority of written accounts, Elsie Frankfurt is given credit for introducing yoga to her sisters and then to the Page Boy plant. However, more than likely Louise Frankfurt Gartner was the sister who actually brought the benefits of yoga to the attention of her sisters and then encouraged them to initiate yoga exercises as a way to bring a relaxation time into the plant. This opinion is supported by interviews with both Louise Gartner, her daughters Gigi and Brenda, and Penny Pollock, Elsie Frankfurt's stepdaughter. According to Penny, Louise was interested in many forms of healthy living from the time she was very young, and she continued that interest into her nineties. However, as it was at other times, it was easier for Elsie—who was always the one being interviewed—to take credit for bringing yoga into the Page Boy plant than it was to give credit to one of her sisters.

A few years later David R. Brown of the *Wall Street Journal* also wrote an article about exercise and how it could release tension. This article, which was directed to executives, touted the benefits of regular, scheduled exercise. Brown also addressed the need for convenient places to work out and promoted the new phenomenon of having gymnasiums or jogging trails near workplaces. Brown even mentioned that he knew one executive who spent a few minutes each day standing on his head. This executive, however, did not promote an exercise break or meditation time for his employees, and unlike the idea promoted at Page Boy, Brown focused his article solely on the benefits of exercise for executives—not for employees.[34]

Even with support from some company executives and enthusiastic journalists, stress-relieving breaks did not become popular during the 1960s.[35] However, the attitude changed in the 1980s as a few executives began to promote "wellness" in their companies. According to Pam DeCastro, a correspondent for the *Boston Business Journal*, by the mid-1980s some New England employers had become concerned about their workers' health. In fact, 62 percent of the firms surveyed for her article indicated that they had implemented programs to improve workers' health. These firms offered a variety of programs, including nutrition counseling, aerobics, yoga, and flexibility training along with lifestyle lectures.[36] Edna, Elsie, and Louise definitely were ahead of the times when they offered yoga as a stress-relieving activity in 1963. Although this practice was a standard daily activity during the 1960s, and the sisters continued to mention it for several years, it is unclear how long the practice lasted. Nevertheless, the Frankfurts were pioneers in the area, and it took more than twenty years for other executives to see that a healthy employee was a productive employee and that a stress-free environment promoted good will and even improved productivity.

Looking back from the twenty-first century, that Page Boy introduced a yoga break and encouraged all workers to participate does not sound unusual. Today companies allow and even encourage workers to maintain healthy lifestyles and to work out and practice relaxation methods. Employers are even required to provide desks that maintain posture and comfort. Large factories and office buildings often house workout facilities and hire specialists to provide lectures about healthy living. However, in the 1960s, the actions taken by the owners of Page Boy were unusual. Indra Devi wrote that she herself had searched for a business with a pioneering spirit willing to create a healthy environment for its employees. In her book she emphasized that she had approached several large firms. She had participated in press conferences and presented lectures, but she had received only vocal support. United Press International ran a favorable article about one of her demonstrations. The executives of Prentice-Hall Publications willingly stretched out on the floor with her and experienced what they said was a wonderful program, but the firm did not opt to initiate the yoga break. Although it is possible that in the 1960s other companies did incorporate relaxation techniques or regular exercise into the work day, no record of such a program was found. Most likely, no large manufacturing concern even considered implementing such a practice. Only three pioneering women from Texas, innovators to the core, were willing to initiate a yoga break at their factory.

The same year that the Frankfurt sisters began their yoga breaks in the factory, a trade journal hailed the sisters as "trailblazers" because of their dynamic and inventive styles and business acumen.[37] This statement was a perfect description of how the sisters operated, and it indicated that others believed that they took imaginative steps both in designing maternity clothes and in creating their advertisements. Elsie was constantly looking for novel ways to advertise, and in November of 1961, Page Boy placed an advertisement in the New Yorker. One sleek black-and-white New Yorker–type drawing showed four men all admiring a svelte woman in a simple empire-waist dress. The caption at the top of the page said, "Why the Admiring Eye?" At the bottom was the Page Boy name and the small trademark logo with the words "Page Boy, That's Why." Further copy said, "All the husbands, including hers, think she looks divine in Page Boy's unexpected fashions for expectant ladies."[38] Then in February 1963 Page Boy styles were highlighted in a three-page spread in Ebony magazine. The article featured Colette (Madame Claus Gerwin), a Paris runway model for high-fashion houses such as Dior, Patou, Rouff, and No-vak. Colette, who was pregnant herself, was photographed wearing a wide range of Page Boy fashions, from a sporty blouson play outfit to a se-quined top over a dinner skirt. The fitted skirt used the new stretch inset at the top of the skirt, and each description mentioned that the fashions were made by Page Boy.[39]

According to author and historian Nancy Walk-er, *Ebony*, which began publishing in 1944 and car-ried stories about prominent African Americans, usually used the same advertisements as publica-tions directed mainly at white readers. This adver-tisement featuring a black model was created to ap-peal to *Ebony* readers. Whether the spread about Colette was an advertisement or a feature article could be debatable. Nevertheless it did advertise clothes because she was photographed in multiple outfits, and the article named the manufacturer, Page Boy.[40]

Page Boy advertisement from *New Yorker*, 1961

Chapter 5

Expanding Horizons, Women's Rights, and a New Life for Elsie

n their designs and in the management of their business, the three sisters proved to be self-directed, innovative, and unconventional. They competed with the larger manufacturing concerns and large department stores. However, even though they accomplished great success, they experienced discrimination in how they were treated or viewed by some business writers, such as Marjorie Farnsworth and the other writers who covered Elsie's induction into the Young Presidents' Organization.

As a result of the sisters' experiences and because Page Boy was owned and run by women and employed mostly women—as most clothing manufacturing businesses in Dallas did—Elsie Frankfurt developed strong feelings about the cultural and legal restrictions imposed on women, and she candidly expressed feminist ideas about women's rights and equality.

As perhaps a first step in making her opinions about women's rights known, Elsie agreed to return to New York in 1958 to appear on the television program *Night Beat: Probe*, hosted by John Wingate. The night's agenda focused on "The Unemancipated Sex." Elsie appeared with two other women, and she explained that women—especially married women—suffered under legally imposed restrictions on their rights and their freedoms.[1]

Elsie continued to develop these feminist ideas, and in 1964 she was interviewed by Pat Herman for a *Family Weekly* article on women as second-class citizens. Herman interviewed four women: Senator Margaret Chase Smith, Judge Anna Kross, Elsie Frankfurt, and Representative Katherine St. George.

It is important to note that three of the women who were interviewed with Elsie worked in government—two in the legislative branch and one in the judiciary branch. Elsie was the lone representative from the private sector and from business.

Herman began her article with a statement from President Kennedy's Commission on the Status of American Women, which had declared that "in every state, married women suffered under disabilities that limited their rights." Herman then asked each of the women whether they had experienced any discrimination themselves, and each woman commented on how they personally had been affected by some aspects of the restrictions on women's rights. Elsie, as the only one of the women who actually employed other women, stated that "the whole concept of special labor laws for women is nonsense and totally unfair."[2] She continued her comments with a question:

> What protection do the women workers in my factory have that the men don't have also? The laws are not protecting women but instead restricting them. There is no substitute for equal rights. . . . I live in a state where my sister had to go into court and ask a judge to remove the "disabilities" she suffered as a married woman before she could come into our business.
>
> Only when her rights as a "feme sole"—single woman—were restored by the court could she become a partner in our business.
>
> But first she had to get her husband's consent,

as she still does if she wants to invest (spend) any of her own money! There are so many discriminations against married women in Texas that it gives a girl good reason to remain single.[3]

Reflecting on this statement and understanding the restrictions that Edna had been forced to overcome in order to carry out normal business activities, that Elsie had not married is not surprising. As a strong-minded woman, she did not want her rights and desires to be subordinated to those of a man—even if that man was her husband.

By the middle of the decade, Page Boy was still quite profitable, and each of the sisters earned a comfortable living from the company; however, it was no longer growing exponentially. According to a financial statement dated December 1963, the company was valued at about $1 million. It held approximately $200,000 in fixed assets and $200,000 in investments, along with about $150,000 in accounts receivable and $100,000 in inventory. As had been the policy, Page Boy had no long term debt—only current accounts payable. Financial documents indicate that the company had been incorporated in 1949. Strangely, the balance sheet and accompanying papers did not list Louise Frankfurt Gartner as a shareholder; instead they stated that current shareholders were Miss Elsie Frankfurt and Mrs. Edna Ravkind, along with Mrs. Jenny Frankfurt, who owned some of the stock but was not active in the business. At the time these documents were assembled, Page Boy employed between 125 and 150 employees a month working in the plant. The company also employed one fulltime sales representative in the New York showroom and one who worked in the Dallas sales office. In 1962 Page Boy had created Page Boy Properties Inc. as a Texas real estate holding company. Page Boy also owned several subsidiary corporations that controlled regional Page Boy outlets. None of these legal documents mentioned Louise Frankfurt Gartner, who was still active in the company, but she must have either never actually owned a share in the company, or she had liquidated her ownership interest before this date.[4]

Perhaps as a way of diversifying their assets, around 1963 the sisters began investing in real estate. As part of the diversification, Page Boy Corporation participated with several other corporations in purchasing thirteen acres of Dallas property. The plot was bounded by Northwest Highway, Hillcrest, and Turtle Creek and was in the area being developed as prime commercial real estate, near what was to become NorthPark Shopping Center.[5]

With the company in a strong financial position but not growing, Elsie needed greater challenges. She had remained active in the Young Presidents' Organization since she joined a decade earlier, and now she became involved in other national business and governmental organizations. The Small Business Administration, a federal government agency, gathered a group of well-known business representatives to travel around the world in search of places that were ripe for business development. Elsie Frankfurt, along with five other businessmen, had been selected as part of a six-person fact-finding mission that was sent to Tunisia. The newly reorganized Agency for International Development focused not on military aid but on long-range economic assistance. Leaders from the agency believed that the American government could better serve the African nations by actually sharing American business knowledge, rather than just transferring money to the government. After Elsie and her travel companions arrived in Tunis and got settled, they were supplied with their own individual drivers so that each person could travel around the city separately. Each committee member focused on specific areas of business, and each traveled with a photographer and an interpreter. During the week-long trip, Elsie and the five men visited various factories, shops, textile mills, and some outlying areas along the Mediterranean Sea. The group met with Tunisian officials to exchange ideas and to gather more information. Elsie was selected to evaluate textile and fashion-related industries, and she visited small shops and textile mills. After a thorough study she determined that the country—which was underdeveloped—was not ready for a joint venture with American fashion designers because Tunisian businessmen did not have access to raw materials. She believed that at the time of the visit any manufacturing that could be planned would need to be done with imported fibers and fabric. She did, however, believe that manufacturing might be possible in the future after Tunisia began manufacturing its own textiles.

Elsie also spent several days studying the Tunisian business model, which intrigued her because her Tunisian contact explained that workers and employers did not negotiate written contracts. Instead all interaction was guided by religious (Muslim) law, which bound the owners to treat the workers fairly. During her visit she picked up some fashion ideas and a few pieces of jewelry that she intended to use as inspiration for Page Boy styles. Stepping outside her specific area of expertise, Elsie fell in love with the unspoiled beaches and noted in her report that they appeared to be ripe for development as resorts. After the eight-day visit, the group returned to Washington, D.C., where they reported to the Agency for International Development.[6]

In June of 1964, Elsie received a letter from Eugene P. Foley, the administrator of the Small Business Administration. The letter thanked Elsie for her service to the country. He continued: "Top officials at the Agency for International Development, the Department of State and the Department of Commerce, as well as other high-level observers of the international and financial scenes, have now been persuaded of the importance and effectiveness of investment missions . . . in Tunisia." Foley then echoed the Kennedy speech and said that Elsie had responded to the call as she worked for her country.[7]

Several journalists covered the trip and reported that throughout the journey, Elsie was dressed in a wardrobe based on her new "Lotus" designs. In explaining the idea of the Lotus dresses, she claimed that she had a flash of inspiration while standing on her head. And between 1963 and 1964 she had become fascinated by skirts that were split but looked like dresses. She designed these outfits so that she could exercise and look pert and fashionable all at the same time. Her idea was that the bodice would be slightly elongated so that it tapered loosely past the waist hitting below the waist at about the top of the hipbone. This gave the wearer enough room to be comfortable, and the elongated bodice gave a long lean line. The Lotus bodice was attached to a full divided skirt. This outfit differed from culottes since Elsie lowered the crotch in her styles and widened each pant leg so the finished garment appeared to be a skirt. Finally, each bottom was attached to a bodice, creating the look of a dress, or if a blouse was worn under the outfit, it would look like a jumper. Every dress included large patch pockets that were fitted with zippered inner pockets that were "pickpocket proof." Elsie thought that these compartments could hold money, keys, and a passport, negating the need for a purse. After wearing the test garments on her trip to Tunisia, she decided to test out the fashion innovation by planning a whirlwind travel event, again wearing only Lotus designs.[8]

This time Elsie planned an around-the-world trip. Using her new innovative design, she created lightweight clothes and packed a wardrobe weighing only ten pounds. She included only Lotus[9] dresses on the trip, and all the designs were created from then new synthetic fabrics, such as the improved Orlon and DuPont's Dacron combinations. Elsie wrote regular newspaper columns about her trip, and in each article she noted not only the design she was

Elsie's early Lotus design, ca. 1964

back Lotus dress. She added that she had even ridden a camel while wearing the split skirt. When she reached Rome and Paris she continued to wear only Lotus outfits. She even wore a formal Lotus design to an embassy ball hosted by the American ambassador to Italy. When she toured France, she continued to wear clothes from her ten-pound Lotus wardrobe. Writing that the French do "NOT encourage any import[ed] fashions," she pointed out that despite this predilection, she had been invited to show her wardrobe on French TV.[10]

Earlier that year Elsie had been approached by DuPont to produce a dress to be worn by the hostesses for the DuPont pavilion at the World's Fair. Always eager for attention, she agreed. The uniform was made from DuPont's new stretch Dacron/cotton/Lycra fabric. Sticking to her new-found design, Elsie created a Lotus dress to fit the needs of the hostesses. Instead of the customary patch pockets, this garment had hidden inset pockets sewn into the seams so they could be closed with zippers.[11]

On one of her regularly planned visits to New York, Elsie attended a performance of the play "Jenny." The star, Mary Martin, had heard that Elsie Frankfurt was in the audience and invited her to come backstage. The two Texas belles had never met, but they quickly realized that they had much in common and became friends. Martin also invited Elsie to visit her in her apartment. When Elsie showed up in a Lotus jumper dress, Martin was intrigued. She thought that the dress looked like her costume from "The Sound of Music" and asked Elsie to explain the

wearing but also the fabric she had used to create the outfits. She wrote, for example, that in Japan she wore an Orlon-jersey Lotus design with a Dacron blouse, simultaneously advertising her own designs and the DuPont fabrics. In India she mentioned purchasing Indian cotton for some of her future Lotus designs, but she continued to advertise DuPont fabrics by saying that she had traveled in the ninety-degree heat wearing a DuPont Dacron-and-cotton low-

WORLD'S FAIR DRESS

Miss Elsie Frankfurt, Dallas designer of Lotus divided skirt fashions, has created this new version, the World's Fair Dress in DuPont's new stretch Dacron/cotton/Lycra fabric in beige, turquoise or green bound in black or in black bound in brown. The added feature is the big hidden "pickpocket" pocket with tasseled zipper for carrying endless items.

Newspaper clipping of Elsie modeling Dacron World's Fair uniform, 1964

concept. Now a captive audience for Elsie's advertisement, Martin listened to all the advantages—it kept the look of a small waist but was loose enough to be comfortable, and it provided the look of a skirt with the advantages of slacks. Although Martin generally only wore clothing made by her own designer, she asked whether Elsie would make a traveling wardrobe for her based on the Lotus design. She ordered several dresses in various styles and lengths. True to her usual ploys, Elsie convinced Martin to appear in at least one photograph taken in her New York apartment.[12] Clearly Page Boy and Lotus profited from Elsie's charm and grace and perhaps even from her Texas drawl and Southern politeness.

Bergdorf Goodman believed in the divided- skirt idea and filled their Country & Casual Shop with the style. They ordered dresses in black and white gingham with collars and shiny black belts, and some with inverted pleats. Some styles for younger clients came in white dotted swiss trimmed with black velvet. The fashions made from more delicate fabrics were lined so that they were opaque and women would not need to wear camisoles under the garments.[13] Although most of the styles were sleeveless, Lotus made some long-sleeved versions in easy-care nylon jersey. One particular style consisted of a tiered skirt that created a ruffled effect, but the lower tier could zip off to convert the long skirt to a short skirt. Prices ranged from $30 to $135.[14] Elsie even made a few "little Lotus" designs. These outfits were created for young girls and preteens.[15] Lotus designs and advertisements appeared for several years and then disappeared by about 1970. Elsie's new creation was eventually killed off by the pants suit, double knits, and the Mod look. Her fashions had always been feminine, and even when shifts and A-line dresses were the rage, Elsie herself preferred to show off her tiny waistline and perfectly proportioned body. The loss of the business was hardly devastating since Elsie had gone on to another life—marriage.[16]

Elsie always wanted to promote both herself and her ideas, and she often created her own opportunities for advertising. For example, in one advertisement for Chesterfield cigarettes, she was photographed in one of her Lotus designs, smoking a long cigarette. The heading for this publicity campaign read, "Chesterfield People: They like a mild smoke, but just don't like filtered. (How about you?)" At fifty-four Elsie looked like a petite blond model, not a tough-minded businesswoman. This advertising campaign also included photographs with Elsie of actors and celebrities such as Ronald Reagan and Byron Harvey, grandson of Fred Harvey, who owned the Harvey House hotels and restaurants.[17]

During the mid-1960s, Page Boy was still adding more outlets, and it opened another Dallas retail outlet in 1965. Again physical location was crucial, and this shop was opened in the upscale NorthPark shopping mall. Neiman Marcus was one of the anchor stores, and Stanley Marcus admitted that he had always wanted to carry the Page Boy line but had never been able to persuade the Frankfurt sisters to allow Neiman's to carry their line. The sisters continued to reject his overtures because they did not want to dilute their Dallas customer base but wanted to capitalize on the traffic created by the Neiman Marcus name. Although they rejected Marcus's offers for Neiman Marcus to carry the line, they usually placed their shops near his upscale stores; this location in NorthPark continued that strategy.

Fitted out with crystal chandeliers and velveteen chairs, the NorthPark shop set the stage for a luxurious shopping experience in the third Dallas outlet. Edna and Louise returned from another trip to Mexico just in time for the opening of the new store. While on this trip they had vacationed and gathered ideas for new styles. Elsie too had been traveling, and she had just returned to Dallas from the Far East. Despite all the traveling, all three sisters were on hand for the opening of the new store and the grand opening of the mall itself. At this time newspaper reports indicated that Page Boy sold about $2.5 million of merchandise a year.[18]

Over the years each of the Frankfurt sisters had developed her own characteristic style, and each sister dressed fashionably and looked distinctive. They always matched their shoes and purse to the outfit they wore and even coordinated their jewelry with the dress they wore to work each day. Although they did not usually wear hats when they went to the office, the sisters always wore stockings and high-heeled shoes. Additionally, both Elsie and Louise emphasized their small waists by using wide belts to cinch in the dress or skirt.[19] To enhance their travel appearances, the sisters all purchased custom-made luggage. And to bring attention to themselves, they also traveled in coordinating outfits made of the same fabric as the luggage. Furthermore, the sisters often wore custom-made shoes that matched the dresses or suits.[20]

By the end of the year, Elsie was off again to Tunisia. This time the American government itself asked her to revisit the country. On this trip she served as a goodwill ambassador. She accompanied several others who were also serving as cultural and goodwill ambassadors. The U.S. government was sending artists—primarily dancers and musicians—along with the ever-charming Elsie. She, rather than a man, had been selected to represent business. The trip paid dividends for both Elsie and Tunisia when six months later Page Boy and the NorthPark developer sponsored a special trade exhibit, "Tunisia in Texas." For the opening of the exhibit, the Tunisian ambassador visited Dallas, and Elsie served as his host.[21] Although Page Boy was not using Tunisian fabrics, she could still promote Tunisian goods.

After several trips either representing the United States government or serving as a quasi-governmental ambassador, Elsie started to show an interest in governmental affairs. Earlier in 1966 she had hosted the benefit style show of the Preston-crest Republican Women's Club in Dallas. Elsie provided the fashions—both Lotus and Page Boy—and was the commentator for the fashion show that raised funds for the Republican Women's scholarship fund.

In September of 1967, *Good Housekeeping* ran an article about women millionaires. The article highlighted six women and included Elsie Frankfurt. The women were described as very feminine, attractive, happy and "all under fifty." (Elsie was a whiz at hiding her age, because she was now well over fifty.) The article described Elsie's life style and her thoughts about marriage. "While her friends were marrying and having children," she "was working twelve hours a day and traveling eight months a year." Now in her mid-forties, according to the article, Elsie said that business success had cut down her chances for marriage. "A male executive can marry his secretary, but the successful businesswoman can only make a happy marriage with a man who is eminent in his own right."[22]

Elsie had expressed her thoughts on marriage in several other articles that also described her luxury-filled life. She told a writer for *Look* that her life was "grand." She spent very little on living expenses since she still technically lived with her mother in Dallas, and Page Boy paid her travel and living expenses while she was in New York.[23] In fact, according to one of her nieces, Elsie's designer clothes were also purchased with company funds, so she spent very little of what she earned on anything except her personal luxuries such as furs.[24]

Elsie added that she had five or six regular "gentlemen friends in New York" and that they always insisted on paying when they took her out during her visits to New York. She also admitted that she had come close to marriage several times but "something . . . always held her back." She liked living large, shopping in designer salons, and eating at El

Morocco. Rhetorically she continued, "You are going to take me out of this great big pond and put me in the little bowl? . . . No, Sir."[25] She did not want to end up in a little pond. Ironically, the interviews for this article, like the one printed in *Good Housekeeping*, must have taken place many months earlier since in June of 1966 Elsie announced that she would wed industrialist Franklin B. Pollock.

The courtship between Elsie Frankfurt and Franklin Pollock had been a whirlwind event for a woman who had been convinced that she did not need a man in her life and who always wanted to remain her own boss.[26] Franklin and Elsie met at a dinner party on a Wednesday; he called on Thursday and sent flowers. She agreed to a dinner date that night during which he announced, "I'm going to marry you." She was convinced he was a kook. He called her again on Friday and invited her to his estate in Westchester County. She agreed—but only if he would get her back to the city by evening because she already had an evening date with someone else. Each day that she remained in New York, Franklin sent flowers to her suite in the Pierre Hotel. He convinced her to accompany him to an upcoming lunch date with another couple. Several days later, Frank had his chauffeur pick her up at the hotel. On their way to the lunch, they stopped at Van Cleef, and then at Harry Winston; from there they went to Cartier and finally stopped at Tiffany. Elsie stayed in New York two weeks, and when she returned to Dallas, she sported a ten-carat canary-yellow diamond on her finger and was ready to announce her engage-ment.

Franklin Pollock was no secretary. Like Elsie he was a self made man, but his wealth had grown well beyond what she could imagine for Page Boy. He began his career as a salesman but eventually worked his way up to become president and chief executive of Thatcher Glass. He also served on the board of directors of several other firms.

When Elsie returned to Dallas, one of her friends suggested that she run a Dun and Bradstreet rating on Franklin Pollock. She thought it over and decided that she needed more information about Pollock and followed her friend's advice. After all, Franklin had already been married four times, and in 1966 he had custody of two young children, a daughter, Penny, and a son, Bobby. While she was still in Dallas, he called her and chided her about losing money on one particular business move she had made. She paused and then retorted, "So you ran a D&B on me?" He had to admit that indeed he had done a bit of snooping. She then quietly revealed to him that she had already run one on him also.[27] This story remained one of the favorite family anecdotes about the couple.

For her wedding Elsie wore a Lotus design in champagne brocade. The outfit consisted of a long-skirted dress with a matching jacket. She also packed thirty Lotus costumes for the honeymoon trip, which included stays in London, Paris, the Rivera, and Tunisia—her favorite country outside Europe. For fifty-five-year-old Elsie—who still claimed to be in her forties—marriage meant that she would need to rearrange at least part of her life. Now, instead of spending most of her time on business, dividing her weeks between Dallas and New York City, and making her own schedule, Elsie had to arrange her days so that she could spend time with her husband and his family. So she added Rye, New York, to her schedule of stops that included New York and Dallas and would very soon include Beverly Hills, California, where the couple moved. Elsie still managed to be present for the seasonal Page Boy showings in New York and to travel back and forth to Dallas when needed. Nevertheless, part of her life had changed. She now had a husband with whom to share her life, and the husband came along with two young children, both of whom needed her attention.

In an interview conducted after Elsie and Franklin married, columnist Martin Abramson said that "with the approval of her husband, Elsie is continuing her business career by transferring some of her administrative functions to Page Boy's New York office," although she was continuing to use her maiden name. One wonders what changed Elsie from someone who wanted to determine her own future and make her own decisions to someone who would allow herself to be guided by "the approval of her husband." Elsie still made trips to Dallas, but they were shorter in duration, and her trips around the country to Page Boy outlets were coordinated to coincide with Pollock's own business trips. She was determined to remain active in Page Boy, but she correlated her own business travel with her husband's travel. Elsie explained that remaining active in Page Boy was part of her self-expression and contributed to her pride of achievement—in effect it was part of her identity.[28] One also wonders why she told a reporter that she would request the approval of her husband when making the decision to remain active in the business—consulting him yes, but asking his approval?

For the next decade Elsie remained very involved in Page Boy management and continued to be quoted in numerous publications. Although for the first several years after her marriage, she used her maiden name exclusively, within a few years she began adding Franklin's name to hers. After all, Franklin Pollock was wealthy—much wealthier than Elsie—and he was well known in the business world. Thus, she was not giving up anything when she became Elsie Frankfurt Pollock because everyone knew who she was, and she gained the status and prestige of being Mrs. Franklin Pollock.

Late in the 1960s the maternity and fashion industry were finding growth and expansion difficult. In the fall of 1967, fashion headlines across the country proclaimed, "Maternity Wear Jolted: Young Mothers-to-Be Get By with Tent Dresses." This headline was not written by a fashion writer but instead by a business journalist, Karol Stonger. In an article about the business of maternity fashion, Stonger said that mothers-to-be were either not purchasing any new maternity outfits or were buying their clothes in the regular ready-to-wear departments. All the maternity manufacturers were hurting. Albert Nipon, who owned the maternity line Ma Mere, said,

"The tent cut into our sales tremendously." He continued, "We created a monster that came back to haunt us." Elsie reported, "The tent affected the entire industry without a doubt."[29] Edna's daughter-in-law remembered that this was a time of stress in Edna's life as she and Elsie fretted over the downturn in business.[30] But Page Boy was still able to maintain sales equal to the those of the previous year.

Chapter 6

Motherhood, In and Out of Fashion

Faced with a difficult business climate, the working arrangement among the sisters began to change. Over time Louise Frankfurt Gartner's husband expressed reluctance for her to be at the factory from early in the morning until late in the evening. Moreover, Louise did not like being away from her home and family all day every day. By 1968 her oldest daughter was twenty, her son was seventeen, and her baby was nine. With the encouragement of her husband, she decided that she wanted to stop working and spend more time at home. Although Louise's name had occasionally appeared in stories during the later years of the 1960s, by 1970 her name had disappeared entirely from all Page Boy publicity. She left the firm, leaving the business to Edna and Elsie.[1] Although Louise had merely retired from business after twenty-five years of work, it seemed that she had been erased entirely from the Page Boy company history. After she left, few stories ever mentioned her name or her contribution to the firm.

As the American fashion industry expanded, Page Boy's management realized that it now had many significant competitors—competitors who were both manufacturing and marketing maternity clothes. Some of these competitors manufactured and sold moderately priced clothing and focused on sporty designs, while others like Albert Nipon introduced a more upscale fashion line. Page Boy was now facing competition on all fronts. First, many more firms had entered the maternity market. These manufacturers were both creating and manufacturing maternity clothes, which they sold to retailers. Second, on the retail level Page Boy now faced competition from chain department stores with maternity departments that could be found in the ever-increasing number of suburban malls. Moreover, Page Boy competed with other specialty maternity boutiques that sold in upscale shops. Although Page Boy sold to some department stores, it carefully limited the department stores that were allowed to carry Page Boy clothes to those with fashionable reputations and those that did not directly compete with Page Boy's own shops.[2] The proliferation of new large chain outlets and small maternity boutiques left Page Boy without a single advantage. And by the end of the 1970s, the enthusiasm for Page Boy clothes that had been transmitted from the original customers to their daughters had begun to wane.[3] Moreover, the birthrate that had hit an all-time high of twenty-five births per one thousand women shortly after World War II soon started declining and continued to decline through the 1960s. It had hit a low of about twenty births per thousand women by 1970.[4]

Page Boy faced another challenge to sales volume besides competition and the decline in the birthrate. Although women were entering the work force in ever-increasing numbers, lifestyles were changing, and even working women's wardrobes were changing. Offices were less formal than they had been in the 1950s and 1960s. Secretaries wore dresses, not suits, to work, and even attorneys could appear in court in a dress rather than a business suit. Stay-at-home mothers no longer dressed in hose and high-heel shoes each day, and even when they went out to meetings, they wore less formal clothing. Women who attended club meetings or went out to play cards no longer wore suits, hats, and gloves to their gatherings. Furthermore, fewer women either wanted to get "dressed up" regularly or needed to get "dressed up" as often as they had in previous decades. The increase in the middle-class made more women capable of purchasing consumer goods, but these women did not share the same life style or fashion rules as their mothers. Comfort was important. Fewer events required dress garments. The lines between work clothes and casual outfits began to blur. Thus, the need for maternity clothes—even for professional women and working women—changed. Finally, and perhaps most importantly for Page Boy, although in earlier decades "a well-dressed woman always" bought the "best quality item" she could afford, by the mid-1970s women began purchasing more outfits and garments, sacrificing quality for quantity. So too in respect to the shopping habits of pregnant women, quantity won out over quality.[5] And quality had been the force guiding manufacturing decisions for both Edna and Elsie throughout the existence of Page Boy.[6] All these situations put downward pressure on Page Boy profits.

By the end of 1970, however, optimism in the maternity fashion business sprang anew. While loosely fitted garments, and especially garments that stood away from the body, were still popular, the tent dresses faded from the fashion scene. Fashion gurus and designers no longer dictated one look for a fashion season or one color as "the" color. Dress lengths varied from outfit to outfit. Everything was "in" except the conventional suits and fitted shirtdress that

Else favored for herself. Pants suits were popular, and skirt lengths ranged from short skirts to ankle lengths. Page Boy followed the trends, showing loosely fitted dresses. These styles were completely alien to both Edna and Elsie, but traces of Elsie's style ideas continued to appear in some of their designs. She added belts to many of the Page Boy fashions. On some of these garments she placed belts above the waist. On others the designers added the suggestion of a belt stitched around the back. Other Page Boy styles were cut with empire waists fitted under the bust. Fashionable fabrics included many synthetics. Styles ranged from dresses with solid skirts and plaid bodices to all-over plaids trimmed in black leather. Jumpers were returning, shown with or without blouses. Most garments had some kind of trim: buttons, belts, laces, and for evening they sparkled with sequins. The Frankfurt sisters favored colors, so Page Boy continued to manufacture its designs in a vast array of colors. Page Boy even came out with a variety of pants suits. Reflecting Elsie's travel influences, the suits varied in their fashion references, with some sporting long Edwardian jackets and others designed with Nehru collars. Fashion writers repeatedly described the modernization in styles even in maternity clothing.[7]

Journalist Richard Baskin noted that specialty maternity shops were increasing in number and opening in both large and small malls across the nation. They could even be found in small neighborhood shopping centers. Importantly, these shops not only carried their own brand of maternity clothing,

Ethnic prints from Page Boy catalog, undated

but they also specialized in many other items needed by pregnant women, new mothers, and newborn infants. These new stores were broadening their appeal by offering a wider range of products and by enticing customers to enter the shops even after the babies were born. Even as Page Boy tried to cope with the newer styles, it fell behind in marketing to mothers-to-be because it focused only on clothing and some fashion items for the pregnant woman. Baskin did give a nod to Page Boy, writing that "the first of the maternity-fashion chains dates back 32 years to a Dallas hayloft rented by two sisters named Frankfurt," but he did not detail what Page Boy was currently showing. He listed instead some of the other and now more forward-looking brands that were serving the California market, including Dorothe Maternity, which opened in 1949 and served California women with thirteen stores, and Motherhood Maternity Shops, which had spread across the West and by 1971 had 100 outlets.

Shares of Motherhood Maternity, which had begun as a privately held company but had recently gone public, were selling for about eight dollars each. The infusion of capital enabled Motherhood Maternity to open scores of shops within a short period of time and thus expand its market territory. Page Boy was still selling to the upscale market, but it had a hard time competing with more widely available brands offered by large publicly held businesses.[8] For thirty years the sisters had run their business by the maxim that if they did not have the cash on hand to buy something, or build something, or make a change, they did not do it. This belief had been ingrained in their father who had survived the Depression, and he had instilled his ethos in his daughters. As a result of these convictions, Page Boy never borrowed to grow and never considered going public to raise funds. Limited funds restricted the growth and expansion of Page Boy, but limited funds was not the only thing that limited the growth or size

of the company. Edna and Elsie's reluctance to hire additional managers with real power—a necessity for large firms—kept them small; Page Boy could not outgrow the capabilities of these two aging women.

In July of 1967, Page Boy suffered the loss of one of its longtime employees, comptroller John Hans Fulda. Fulda had been one of the few men besides William Lacky working for Page Boy; he had started working for the company shortly after World War II. Although Fulda was a German refugee who had arrived in the United States in 1939 when he was more than forty, he had earned a degree from Southern Methodist University and had contributed to the business side of the firm.[9] His loss decreased the external influence and intensified the scarcity of independent business expertise.

In what was perhaps a small attempt to compete with the expanding chains, Page Boy purchased an ongoing maternity shop in Kansas City, Missouri. The firm, Frances Welsh Maternity Shop, was about twenty years old. This acquisition, however, added only one outlet to the list of Page Boy shops, and the acquisition did not significantly change the Page Boy marketing reach. The transaction was announced by Page Boy's new executive vice president William Ravkind, Edna's thirty-three-year-old son. John Fulda's death in 1967 had left a vacancy in the business management side of Page Boy, and Ravkind, who had been practicing law in the Dallas area, was recruited to bring youthful energy and stamina into the firm's business management.[10] Page Boy never

Front cover of Page Boy catalog, 1974

publicly announced that Ravkind had joined the firm; instead his name and title just appeared in the announcement of the acquisition of the Kansas City shop. Ravkind only remained with Page Boy for a short time before returning to private practice.

By hiring Ravkind the remaining sisters, Edna Frankfurt Ravkind and Elsie Frankfurt Pollock, indicated that they were looking for someone who could come into the firm and perhaps assist with the everyday, hands-on part of managing the business. Nevertheless, Edna and Elsie placed restrictions on William's authority, especially when it came to upper-level management decisions and particularly in making financial decisions. The sisters still relied on one of their father's admonitions—never borrow money. Unfortunately, this adage, which was good advice in the 1930s and 1940s, was no longer valid. Once William Ravkind had familiarized himself with the financial situation of the firm and understood that his mother and his aunt were unwilling to borrow funds so that the company could grow, he realized that the firm was not large enough to continue enriching the owners and support his ambitions as well. Without borrowing to expand, Page Boy would continue to make his mother and his aunt wealthy, but it would not enrich him.[11]

Furthermore, Edna and Elsie were still dynamic, active businesswomen who had been running Page Boy without much assistance; even though they were each nearing sixty-five, they were not willing to hand over management of the company to a new generation. This fact only became obvious after Wil-

liam Ravkind joined the company. Page Boy was Elsie and Edna's baby, and they saw no reason to allow anyone else to control their creation. According to family members, Edna and Elsie never offered William a contract, and he never asked for or signed a formal agreement with Page Boy—either before he joined the firm or after. Thus, it was only after he began working for Page Boy that he must have realized that this step was ill conceived, ill planned, and ill executed.

Sometime around 1970 Page Boy published a brochure that contained a short history of the firm along with some other information including self-promotion. It began, "Just about every media in our great country has recognized the two Frankfurt sisters." Louise's name never appeared in any part of the story. Edna and Elsie articulated the philosophy behind Page Boy's fashion creations and described their creative process. As Elsie had indicated in many earlier articles, the sisters never tried to create or dictate fashion—they did not want to be innovative or decide what was "in" or "out" of style. Instead, they wanted to create maternity clothes in "the fashion for today's woman [today meaning the current time—whenever that was] in the most modern, realistic, and attractive way" possible. Thus, Page Boy designers never intended to be the creators of the yearly trends or styles. Instead, they wanted to be interpreters of those trends or fashions for the pregnant woman.

The advertising booklet also contained, perhaps for the first time, a description of how Page Boy actually designed and created the clothes it manufactured. "Page Boy clothes didn't just happen—many of our exclusive designs are on the drawing board nine months before the garments are manufactured. Every item tells a story; it all goes together." Often Page Boy manufactured several outfits from the same fabric, making coordinating garments using the same or similar fabrics. In most instances the garments began with the fabric; years earlier Edna had mentioned searching the world over for fabrics that she could collect or bank for future use in Page Boy designs. Because the people who actually created the designs had worked together for many years, they were familiar with each others' work habits, and collaboration was easy. When it was decided that a particular bolt of fabric should be used during a specific season, the designer would drape the fabric over a dress form. This step allowed the designers to see how the fabric would drape and fold and also how it would either cling to or stand away from the human body. After these properties were determined, the designer could imagine a garment made from the fabric and create a design. Next, ideas were worked out on the design board, and only after the design was formalized was the sample cut and assembled. Models tried on the sample garment, and the designer could then see whether changes needed to be made in the way the garment was put together. Often, however, Edna stepped in at this stage and actually tried on the garment herself to see how it felt and moved on her body. When everything was perfect, the final step was taken: the pattern would be

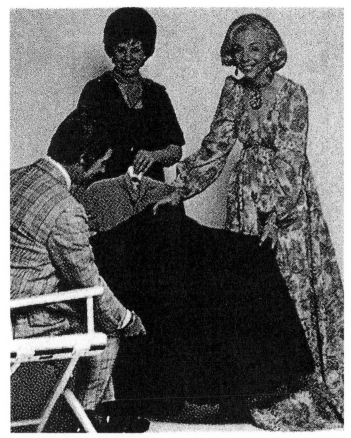

Edna, Marjorie Rubin, and Bill Lackey, ca. mid-1970s

graded and the garment would be made for sale. All the samples, even those that never made it into production, were sold in the Dallas outlet.

Although this booklet was published to sell clothes, it also provided the public with additional information about the inner workings of the firm and contained photographs of both Edna and Elsie, making them more real to customers. And in a nod to two very important employees, it also contained photographs of longtime associates Marjorie Rubin and Bill Lackey.[12] The booklet never mentioned Louise's name or the fact that she had been the chief designer for over two decades.

Despite the fact that Elsie often overshadowed Edna in Page Boy's publicity, Edna often ranked "Number One" within the Ravkind family circle club, "Ravkind Family Inc." The sisters worked together, but Edna socialized more with Abe's family than she did with her own sisters. As one granddaughter said when talking about how often the family gathered together, "The family was not especially close."[13] Conversely, Abe's family regularly socialized with relatives and friends of the Ravkind brothers and sisters. Usually such family circles or clubs were founded by Jewish siblings or cousins who were first-generation Americans born to Eastern European immigrants. Often formed to mitigate assimilation, some also served as ways to provide family-based charity or, as in the Ravkind family, purely as a social organization to hold the family together.[14] Ravkind Family Inc. held monthly meetings, and the location rotated from one family member to another. At these events new members were introduced into the family, and various family milestones were announced. Ravkind Family Inc. planned a yearly gathering at the Baker Hotel in Mineral Wells, Texas, and at one time was collecting money to build a cabin on Grapevine Lake.

Ravkind Family Inc.[15] also sponsored all large family gatherings where family and friends socialized at *simchas*, or celebrations. They also "voted once a year to bestow the highest honor on 'Number One'"—the wackiest or zaniest person in the family. Many family members sought this prize by pulling outlandish stunts on other family members. Always competing vigorously for the prize, Edna often walked away with the title of "Number One." Her daughter Joan recounted one particular summer when her mother campaigned wildly so that she could go home from the reunion at the Baker Hotel with the title of "Number One." "Family Inc. members and friends used to go to Mineral Wells," Joan explained, and on one occasion, while lounging around the pool, "my mother assured her place as Number One." First, Edna gathered the group around the pool, and after she had everyone's attention, including nonfamily members, she led everyone in yoga exercises. To cap this off, she instructed the assembled sun worshipers in how to "sun their tongues." As part of her campaign during that same trip, Edna got "everyone to line up in the hall of the hotel," and providing instructions and demonstrations, she talked everyone into a headstand.[16] Joan described the scene—a group of middle-aged men and women lined up in the hall of the hotel, all standing on their heads.

By 1970 Elsie was facing another challenge in her personal life. During 1969 and 1970 she was flying back and forth between New York and California, checking on the stores in California and then returning to the Pollock home in Westchester County or to her apartment at the Pierre Hotel in New York City. About this time Franklin's company, Thatcher Glass, merged with Dart Industries, and since Dart's headquarters was in California, Franklin decided that he needed to live in California. The couple moved into the Bel Air Hotel while also retaining the property in Westchester County. Elsie, Franklin, and the children talked over the situation and debated whether or not Franklin should keep the New York home to serve the children as their home base. The couple lived in the hotel for about a year until the children assured the couple that they would be happy living in California. Elsie and Franklin bought a house in Holmby Hills, a neighborhood between Beverly Hills and Bel Air, California, that provided privacy, large estates, and proximity to notable people.[17]

After Elsie and Franklin settled into life in Southern California, their names began to appear in the society pages there, and they mingled with many entertainers. Elsie became noted for throwing dinner parties, especially for hosting Sunday night suppers. Ever proud of her Texas roots, Elsie specialized in chili dinners. Although she had a cook and other servants, when she served chili, she made it herself. Jody Jacobs, columnist for the *Los Angeles Times*, de-scribed one of her dinners: "Mrs. Franklin Pollock's chili tastes better each time she serves it. So much so that even Frank, who's not from Texas like his perky wife, finally succumbed and after nine years of marriage, is enjoying the spicy stuff." Jacobs added that the party was such a success that Franklin even stayed up past his 10:30 curfew.[18] A year later Elsie threw another party, and this time she served hamburgers and hot dogs along with cocktails. The guests were entertained with an informal fashion show of Page Boy fashions. The clothing seemed appropriate since Elsie was raising funds for the new Cedars-Sinai maternity ward. Her guests for this event included Cher, Nancy Sinatra, Jayne Meadows Allen, and Florence Henderson.[19] Both Allen and Henderson had previously served as commentators for Page Boy style shows.

Shortly after settling in California, Elsie joined the Women's Guild of Cedars-Sinai Medical Center. She had perhaps grown tired of spending all her energy and time focusing on Page Boy business, or perhaps she wanted an opportunity to socialize with some of the Hollywood royalty. Within a few years she was elected to serve on the board of the 2,000-member organization. She also appeared in many publicity photographs for this and various other charities, and she and Franklin were the subject of several articles in the local newspapers. It was clear that Elsie loved living in California and relished the publicity she received. In addition, Franklin's wealth—which far exceeded her own—enabled her to live in luxury, socialize with famous people, and join any organization she thought might increase her visibility.

Earlier in her life Elsie had traveled around the world for business and pleasure, but after settling in California, she curtailed some of her traveling. Although she still traveled for business within the United States, she significantly reduced her overseas traveling. She and Franklin preferred to stay in Southern California, and she commented that she had had her fill of traveling while she was younger. Now she just wanted to enjoy her home. This comment is not surprising since Elsie had never actually been able to call any of the places she lived "her home." When she had been in Dallas, she lived with her mother, and when she was in New York, she lived in the Pierre Hotel. After her wedding to Franklin, she continued to live in these places and simply added Franklin's house in Rye to the list of borrowed houses. This extremely successful woman had never purchased a home of her own—one that she could decorate—until she was about sixty years old.

In about 1975 Franklin retired from Dart, but at seventy-two he was too restless to give up all business activities. By constantly looking over Elsie's shoulder, he worked his way into the management of Page Boy, and in a surprising move for a self-made, strong-willed woman, Elsie began to defer to Franklin in financial matters relating to Page Boy. In an even more astonishing step, she asked Franklin to oversee Page Boy's finances. He and Elsie worked out a system to keep tabs on Page Boy business while never leaving Southern California. One can only wonder what caused this change in Elsie's ideas about her place in the world and about how a woman might allow a man to manage "her" business—her baby.

After he became involved in Page Boy affairs, Franklin became familiar with each store manager and each store's operating procedures. According to Penny Pollock, Page Boy used a three-section, perforated garment tag attached to each item. This format allowed Elsie and Franklin to keep track of the sales figures for each sales clerk, each store, and each garment style. When an item was sold, one section of the tag would be left on the garment, one section remained in the store where the sale was made, and one section was mailed to Franklin and Elsie in California. Franklin and Elsie would gather all the sales tags and check which styles were selling. On Sunday mornings Franklin would call each store, asking for the week's sales figures. He kept records for each sales associate, recording their numbers for the week, and he recorded the total sales for the store. He could then compare the figures, checking trends to see whether the store was ahead of the previous week's sales figures or behind. He could also keep track of each sales associate. All these figures were kept using the paper garment tag and pencil and paper—without the aid of a computer. After checking in with the store managers and reviewing the figures, Elsie and Franklin could report problems back to the managers. Because of his strict control over the finances and his knowledge of the sales, employees called Franklin "our father who art in California."

By this time Elsie rarely traveled back to Dallas. She did, however, make an appearance at the Wilshire Avenue store and on occasion even assisted customers. She was the consummate sales person, making each customer feel as if she was the center of Elsie's attention. Some customers would even return later, asking about the elegant lady who had waited on them previously. They were always shocked to discover that it had been the owner of the firm.

Elsie was always curious about what the other maternity manufacturers were showing. She wanted to compare the styles and quality of those garments to Page Boy's fashions. This became simpler when Penny, her stepdaughter, became pregnant: like sleuths, they would spend an afternoon going from one maternity store to another, checking out the different styles. Penny tried on many outfits just so they could check the garments out. Once in the dressing room, Penny and Elsie could examine the clothes and see how a style fit and how well it was made. The two thought these excursions were a lark and enjoyed the joke they were pulling on the other firms. They had so much fun that later, when Penny was no longer pregnant, they pretended that she was just so they could continue these excursions. This allowed them to continue playing the sleuth. Elsie had not developed a close relationship with Penny while she was younger, but this ploy bridged the separation and helped her develop a closer relationship with her stepdaughter.[20]

Beginning in the holiday season of 1971, Page

Undated photograph from Page Boy catalog ca. mid-1970s

Boy expanded the offerings in its stores. The company had stopped manufacturing lingerie in the 1960s, but the 1971 holiday advertisements touted the "introduction of a lingerie line." The company also introduced an exclusive line of Page Boy body cream containing cocoa butter, olive oil, and apricot oil. In addition, it began to promote other non-clothing items, including a prenatal pillow with a hollowed-out area that aided the expectant mother when she rested or slept.

Edna believed that Page Boy offered great styles and fashionable accessories, and she and Elsie both claimed that nonpregnant women often shopped in the Page Boy stores, purchasing scarves and other accessories. Edna added her observations, stating that since the 1970s styles for regular ready-to-wear resembled maternity wear and that even women and teenagers who were not pregnant were purchasing high-fashion Page Boy designs. She emphasized that "women and teen-agers find the empire waistlines becoming and fashion-right for today," even though they were not pregnant. The teenagers liked the Page Boy smocks, Edna asserted, whereas the more mature women liked the long, flowing evening gowns.

Edna and Elsie remained the controlling managers of Page Boy, but during the 1970s they began mentioning the names of Bill Lackey and Marjorie Rubin in more of the publicity. For example, one brochure pointed out that "besides the Page Boy founders, Edna Frankfurt Ravkind and Elsie Frankfurt Pollock, the guiding lights at the Dallas home office include Bill Lackey and Marjorie Rubin." Among other jobs Lackey and Rubin were in charge of styling and fabric selection. James Fuller had been hired as the lingerie buyer, but he served double duty and also worked as the fashion consultant handling wholesale customers in the Dallas showroom.[21] These advertisements indicated that the sisters were beginning to need additional managerial-level assistants. But it was also evident that Elsie and Edna were not relinquishing any of their power.

Lackey, who had begun his career as a ballroom dancer and instructor, met Edna when she hired him to give her and her husband dancing lessons. After going to work for Page Boy, he served as Page Boy's general manager and Edna's personal problem solver. He worked in the factory and even traveled for the firm, but he also smoothed over the small tiffs created by Edna's personality. She was quite eccentric, and her abruptness often left enraged waiters and incensed clerks in her wake. Lackey was frequently left to pick up the pieces and smooth the hurt feelings.[22] Even though Edna's family and close friends spoke lovingly of her and talked about how much fun it was to be around her, they all admitted that she could be unconventional. For example, while Edna and Bill Lackey were dining out one day, she asked Lackey to adjust her shoe buckle, expecting him to kneel down and adjust the shoe during the meal.

When Edna traveled, Lackey and Rubin would do all of her packing. When a trip approached, Edna, Marge, and Bill discussed the scheduled events and planned the outfits she would wear each day while she traveled. Then, shortly before she left, Edna would bring all her clothes, shoes, underwear, and toiletries to the office, where either Lackey or Rubin would pack for her. In a few instances the packing was not complete before Edna left on the trip, so Lackey or Rubin would ship the luggage off to her at her destination. Referring to Lackey's unusual list of duties, Edna commented that everyone wanted to be eccentric but only the rich were able to get away with it.[23]

While Lackey and Rubin both served as Edna's personal assistants, the two had very different assignments within Page Boy itself. Lackey had begun as a lower-level employee and become general manager, and Rubin, who had also started her career as a lower-level employee, became the outside buyer and arbiter of style disagreements. Rubin was in charge of purchasing all the trims, buttons, and zippers that were needed in the manufacturing process; she also bought all the other items that were sold in the Page Boy stores, such as stockings, hats, and accessories. These items were manufactured specifically for Page Boy so that the company could claim that they were Page Boy exclusives. Additionally, the sisters felt that they could have some control over the quality and price of items sold in their stores if they had exclusive contracts. Rubin also served as the final vote if there was a style disagreement during the manufacturing process or if one sister favored manufacturing a particular style and one sister did not.

Although Page Boy did not purchase the raw materials to have fabrics made especially for them, it did search for fabrics early in the manufacturing process. Thus, the company was never short on fabric, and by using fabric that it had previously purchased, it could control and accurately predict the cost of garments by using items already on hand. Despite not beginning with the raw materials and being technically a vertical operation, the company purchased and stockpiled the necessary notions and fabrics to use later, avoiding the need to purchase supplies at the last minute. The sisters could calculate the cost as they planned and as the process proceeded. By keeping costs at a predictable level, Elsie and Edna could continue to provide quality garments, just as each had always been determined to do.[24]

As Elsie began cutting back on her travel schedule, Edna began to appear at publicity events for some of the stores. Nevertheless, when there was an opportunity for splashy publicity, Elsie appeared and was still willing to travel. She also continued to make television appearances, and in May of 1974, she appeared on *Dinah's Place,* the talk show hosted by Dinah Shore. Elsie explained how a pregnant woman could plan an entire wardrobe, from bathing suits to casual outfits to long evening skirts, and purchase everything from Page Boy. She pointed out that for 1974 Page Boy was focusing on the "Gatsby look." In reporting on this interview, Harry Bowman, TV editor for the *Dallas Morning News,* wrote that Susan Saint James was expecting again; he commented that Saint James could get some fashion pointers by watching *Dinah's Place* and checking out the Page Boy wardrobe.[25] This was the kind of free publicity that Elsie loved and upon which she had relied from the beginning. But by this time free endorsements were harder and harder to get.

The sisters never considered selling part of the business, taking in additional partners, or even relaxing control over the management of Page Boy. William Lackey's name and photograph, however, began to appear more often in Page Boy promotional materials and in newspaper articles. Lackey even traveled to California to do the commentary for a champagne fashion show to benefit the Hoag Hospital obstetrics department in Newport Beach. Instead of Elsie's appearing in the publicity photographs, Lackey appeared, chatting with benefactors and models showing off Page Boy clothing.[26]

In the early 1970s Page Boy made a major change in its business and merchandising model and ceased all wholesaling of its designs. This decision ended the sale of Page Boy clothing through department store chains such as Lord & Taylor, Saks Fifth Avenue, and Foleys and greatly reduced the number of places where a woman might find Page Boy clothes. This decision also drastically reduced the number of items manufactured. Both sisters claimed that the step was necessary for the survival of the company.

Elsie argued that sales to chain stores were actually a financial burden (rather than a benefit) because large chain retailers often demanded the right to return unsold garments; this system meant that Page Boy was obliged to grant a credit to those stores for the returned merchandise. According to Elsie, such practices harmed Page Boy's bottom line because Page Boy gave a credit to the department store and then needed to dispose of the garments at a discount. The argument completely ignores the volume of sales that accrued through this means of distribution. By not addressing the drastic reduction in the number of garments manufactured and sold, Elsie framed the change in a positive financial light. Her only concession was that there was a reduction in the face-to-face interaction that she and Edna had with the customers, which she regretted.

In taking the credit or blame for discontinuing wholesaling, Edna added, "I stopped it [wholesaling]. Elsie fell in love and I couldn't handle the wholesale end of it."[27] Evidently Edna felt that she had reached the limits of her physical abilities and that she could not handle the workload required to deal with the wholesale customers, while also managing the Dallas stores and the main office. Perhaps this was the first outward crack in the relationship between the two sisters and indicated the limits of their ability to control the company. By now Edna was sixty-seven, and she had been working steadily since she was about twenty. This step, however, could also be seen as foreshadowing the eventual demise of the business twenty years later because the decision closed one revenue stream. It also ended any future option that Page Boy had to switch from retailing through its own outlets to wholesaling through department stores—a change that might have cut down on some management burdens since the firm would only have been responsible for distribution to wholesalers and not running the shops itself.

Even though free publicity about Page Boy decreased, at special occasions Page Boy was still able to garner free publicity and get its name into the newspapers. For the holiday fashion season in 1974, Page Boy announced that it was showing a new concept in holiday styles—the pajama look—certainly not a wardrobe option for professional women. Edna was interviewed about the season's offerings, and she stated that she believed the styles would be "a spectacular line," noting that Page Boy had created pajama fashions for both day and evening. Edna claimed that the new outfits would be created from "the most exciting and feminine fabrics," including crepe de chine and silk matte jersey. Edna concluded the interview by stating that Page Boy had "taken another step ahead," offering "several mix-and-match wardrobes." For the current mothers-to-be this might have been a new idea, but it reprised Page Boy ideas from the 1950s.[28]

The interview also indicated a change in the way that Page Boy publicity was being handled. Elsie was no longer the sole voice and face of the company. Edna was asserting herself, and she began to voice her own opinions and be quoted in print. These changes might also have indicated that tension was continuing between Edna and Elsie. Edna still worked every day at the Dallas office and spent time driving from one Dallas outlet to another, while Elsie was working more sporadically. She and Franklin al-

located Sundays for Page Boy business, but she was no longer focused on the day-to-day management of the company. She was beginning to live another life while Edna was still totally immersed in Page Boy management.

By the early 1970s the Page Boy building was nearly twenty-five years old, and the area around the plant was beginning to look run-down. Moreover, the area was not as fashionable as it had once been. At the same time some Dallas-area manufacturers had already moved to smaller towns around the city, and Edna and Elsie considered moving their plant from the location at Cedar Springs and Olive, just north of the downtown business district, to another location. Making a decision proved difficult, and they wavered back and forth. By 1975 the sisters began to feel that the area around the building was showing some signs of revitalization so they decided to stay where they were. After all, this location was convenient for Edna, who lived a short drive north, and it was within an easy commute for many of the longtime employees.

Edna and Elsie decided to renovate. Staying within the family, they hired their niece, Ethel Frankfurt, an interior decorator, to renovate the building and redecorate the offices. They asked Ethel to evaluate the structure and make some suggestions. Ethel surveyed the premises and decided that the building was structurally sound and only needed cosmetic changes. Probably one of the most foresighted decisions that the sisters had made when the building was originally designed was the decision to air-

Inside the factory, showing the stock of buttons, thread, and trim, undated

Cutting tables, showing pattern layouts and fabric stocks, undated

Dressing Modern Maternity

condition the entire plant. This choice lengthened the life of the building because it did not need retrofitting to add a cooling system.

Since this was a time when colorful clothes were in style, Ethel planned the new showroom to spotlight the colorful clothes. She had the walls painted white, used black and white for the floors and furnishings, and added some silver accents for sparkle.[29] This revitalization created a modern face for Page Boy that lasted until the building was closed and sold.

A few years later Page Boy scored a coup when Elsie convinced Bob Mackie—designer to the stars—to design a line of maternity clothes exclusively for Page Boy. Elsie promised that if Mackie agreed to design the outfits, Page Boy would offer the Mackey designs exclusively in the California stores. Mackie agreed and designed a variety of garments for Page Boy. Each of his outfits included a dramatic tunic of polyester crepe. Some of the tunics were covered with a diaphanous cardigan created from two layers of chiffon. The Mackie outfits included roomy pajama pants with a low-set crotch and an elastic waist, also created from layers of chiffon. Many garments could be worn alone or paired with the tunics or cardigans. Mackie also designed a black polyester chiffon evening gown with an elastic empire waist. Since the designs were created of multiple layers of gossamer fabrics with elastic waists, all the Mackie styles were actually intended to be worn "before, during and after . . . the blessed event." Of course, Elsie saw to it that the article about the designs included information about Mackie's other clients and mentioned that Mackie created all of Cher's TV costumes. Prices for the Mackie garments ranged from $150 to $250, although the small matching scarves that could be used as turbans sold for only $15.[30] These prices would automatically limit the number of women who could afford the items and would make them more appealing to the celebrities and wealthy women who shopped at the Los Angeles stores.

Although Page Boy was no longer "the only place" to shop for maternity clothes, the California shops maintained some name appeal and still attracted customers from the entertainment industry. In a July 1977 interview Elsie announced that Natalie Cole had recently purchased her entire maternity wardrobe from Page Boy. Cole's purchases included everything from bathing suits and short shorts with bare tops to jeans and T-shirts. Elsie also mentioned that Cole had bought evening dresses and pointed out that she appeared at a Muhammad Ali fight in a silver sequin coat and ultrasuede pants that she had purchased from the Page Boy evening collection designed by Bob Mackie.[31]

By 1979 Edna finally admitted in print that she and Elsie did not always agree on fashion choices or the business decisions they needed to make. She even admitted her feeling that she never got as much credit as she deserved for her contribution to the company. She said, though, that their talents "complemented each other." According to Edna, Elsie was especially good at public relations and business, while she herself had an eye for fashion and could manage the tedium of the day-to-day activities of the firm.[32] The last statement about fashion is interesting since Elsie was the sister who bought and wore designer clothes, and it had been Louise and Elsie who had been the original designers for the firm.

The business of designing and manufacturing maternity wear had been a roller coaster ride for years. By the mid-1970s, many department stores had even removed their maternity departments so that they could use the space more efficiently and more profitably. The postwar baby boom had completely disappeared, and by the mid-1970s couples were opting to limit the number of children in their families. Some couples even decided not to have children, a new phenomenon made possible in the previous decade by the widespread availability of birth control.

The slump in sales began to ease in the late 1970s as some women who had postponed having children realized that they could not continue to indefinitely postpone pregnancy. However, one of the main differences between these pregnant women and those of the 1950s and early 1960s was that the women of the late 1970s had planned pregnancies. When pregnancies were planned, the women were more prepared and could afford more upscale clothes. By the end of 1977, half the customers patronizing maternity departments or shops were between the ages of twenty-six and thirty-four. Because they were more financially secure, these women were willing to spend twice as much on a maternity wardrobe as younger customers who had not saved

for the eventual pregnancy. In addition to being more mature, many of the women were working mothers who earned salaries and did not plan to take a leave of absence or give up their careers after they delivered. By the end of the decade, *Business Week* reported that some merchants who had dropped maternity clothing from their divisions were now rethinking that decision. Virginia Cartwright, the bridal and maternity buyer for The Broadway in Los Angeles, said "We're rediscovering maternity wear and expecting a booming market by 1980."

In 1970 first-time births accounted for 38.4 percent of total births, but predictions for 1980 were that this number would rise to 44 percent of all births. The birthrate rose in 1977 to about 3.3 million births annually from 3.2 million the previous year, but it would stay far below the 4.2 million annual births of the baby boom years. More long-range studies predicted that the number of births would reach 4 million annually by 1981, and that the birthrate would remain at that level for most of the 1980s. The rise was significant because many of the pregnant women would be first-time mothers, who could not rely on a maternity wardrobe already in their closets and would be buying a new maternity wardrobe.[33]

One additional change took place in the fashion industry during the later 1970s that helped increase the sales of maternity clothes—styles changed. Whereas women's clothing styles for the late 1960s and shortly thereafter were more loosely fitting, by the end of the 1970s the styles had become more figure hugging. Fashions had swung from hippy to preppy, and blazers and suits had returned to the fashion scene.

With the change in styles, women began to wear shorter skirts with patterned stockings, and even pregnant women were looking for a new style. Believing that these changes would revitalize the maternity wear business, Jerome Rogoway, president of the Motherhood Maternity chain, said that "the maternity business is up for grabs." Anyone would have a chance to make money in the revitalized field. Sears was allocating ten pages in its catalog to maternity clothing, and Lillian Tomack, the buyer for Bloomingdales, noted that department stores were "restocking" maternity departments. Macy's observed that in its California stores sales of maternity clothing had risen 98 percent in 1978; Macy's had also added higher-priced maternity garments to the maternity department. These upscale clothes were flying off the racks; however, Macy's buyers indicated that it was difficult to find and stock fine-quality, sophisticated maternity clothing for the working woman.[34] Macy's and other department stores would have been a perfect place for Page Boy's upscale designs, but unfortunately Page Boy lost this market when it stopped wholesaling.

With the market expanding other companies began entering the field of maternity clothing. Mother Care Ltd., a London-based chain, entered the American market in 1976; by 1978 it had opened 153 shops. Another firm, Dan Howard Industries of Chicago, was opening one outlet every other month. Lady Madonna, which specialized in high-fashion designs, also noted that the customer base had changed. They were serving more working women, who needed business attire, and thus they were adding tweeds and gabardines to their style inventories. All these facts were important to the business of manufacturing maternity clothes, and maternity manufacturers knew that working women spent about $500 on their maternity wardrobes—compared to housewives, who only spent about $350.[35]

For four decades Page Boy had specialized in better-quality—often high-fashion—maternity garments in order to satisfy that niche market. In fact, Marylou Luther, the *Los Angeles Times* fashion editor, wrote a column in 1976, commenting on the lack of good-quality maternity clothes. A reader responded to this article and pointed out that for years Page Boy had been making "great fashion contributions" to the maternity fashion market. Luther replied, "I came, I saw, and now that I'm boned up, here is my public announcement that quality is, indeed, alive and well at Page Boy." The reader signed the response to the column—E.F.P—who was, of course, Elsie Frankfurt Pollock. Luther continued her comments, describing one fashion-forward garment as being created of 100 percent polyester jersey. She noted that the garment sold for $74. Three years later fashion had evolved, and again Page Boy advertised that its clothes were all made from natural fibers—silk, wool, and linen fabrics. When Marylou Luther later responded to a query about "second-class fashion citizens, pregnant women," this time she pointed out that Page Boy was featuring natural fabrics, and she included an illustration of a $125 silk jacquard maternity dress by Page Boy. In this article Elsie was quoted as saying that many manufacturers believed that pregnant women would never spend more than $100 for one maternity garment or outfit, but Page Boy was continuing to make high-quality fashion garments, and for that reason it was the exception and was selling garments at $100 and more.[36]

At the turn of the decade, the *Wall Street Journal* ran an article focusing on the business of manufacturing maternity clothing. Noting that working women were fueling the increase in sales of maternity clothing, the article focused on the top retailers: Motherhood Maternity, which owned 326 shops; Mother Care Ltd., which owned 170 shops; and Lady Madonna, which owned 90 outlets. Motherhood Maternity, like Page Boy, was privately held, but it was expected to do about $34 million in sales for 1979. Mother Care announced that its sales would rise about 32 percent over the previous year, and Lady Madonna, another privately held company, expected sales to reach $20 million—about 33 percent above the previous year's sales. Although Page Boy was mentioned in the article, it was described as a privately owned business with only 30 outlets.[37] In a decade of growth and expansion, Page Boy had hardly grown at all.

This article highlighted Page Boy's unfavorable position compared to other maternity manufacturers. It was being overshadowed by the new compa-nies and outcompeted by even the smallest of the new firms. Although no one actually knew Page Boy's sales figures, fifteen years later Page Boy reported doing about $8 million in sales. Figures would need to be adjusted back, but comparing the 1980 figures of the other firms to the 1993 figures of Page Boy, Page Boy's sales equaled less than one-fifth of what the larger firms were doing. Moreover, the figures might indicate that Page Boy had less than ten percent of the total market. With only two women in complete control of the business, it is doubtful that Page Boy could have handled a large increase in sales—even if Edna and Elsie had tried to increase production.

One might even wonder whether or not there was an increased demand for Page Boy clothes in its own stores. Even if there had been an increase in demand, could Page Boy have increased the production to supply more items to the shops it did have? Finally, location affected the sales numbers. If a woman, especially a busy career customer, ventured into a Page Boy shop and found one or two outfits she liked though she actually needed five, would she return to the Page Boy outlet, or would she choose to shop where there was a larger selection? Probably the latter. Finally, with only thirty Page Boy outlets, women could find other chains within a shorter drive from work or home. Page Boy had closed down its wholesaling division six years earlier and so did not offer its line in department stores such as Lord & Taylor, Saks, or local chains like Foley's or J.W. Robinson's, stores that could be found in many shopping malls. Neither Edna Ravkind nor Elsie Pollock were interviewed for the *Wall Street Journal* article, whereas executives of the three larger maternity firms where all interviewed about their plans for the future and their opinion about the business.

Three years later, the *Wall Street Journal* ran another article about maternity clothes. This time the article focused on the shoppers themselves. A pregnant attorney noted that she could not find suits appropriate for court. Furthermore, she explained that she had shopped in Atlanta, Boston, and Manhattan, and not finding what she needed, she had resorted to ordering her clothes from Mothers Work, which at the time was only a catalog business located in Philadelphia. An obstetrician who also happened to be pregnant herself said she planned to keep the Mothers Work catalogs in her waiting room. Another woman said that she had been forced to shop in a boutique and had paid $300 for one suit so that she could "continue looking professional while pregnant." She did note that she was surprised to find "a lot of designer names you see when you're not pregnant" showing garments at that store.[38] All these women were looking for the kind of clothing that had made Page Boy famous in the 1950s and 1960s. Unfortunately, either these women believed that Page Boy no longer manufactured the type of garments they needed, or the Page Boy shops were not available to these women.

Although the number of babies born in 1957 and the number predicted to be born in 1987 were the same, the continued increase in the number of first-time mothers had a positive effect on the sales of maternity clothes and baby accessories because first-time mothers always spent more on clothes and baby accessories than those women who already had a child. In 1957 about 27 percent of births were to first-time mothers, whereas in 1980 that number had risen to 43 percent—or nearly half of all births—and the number continued to rise. First-time mothers need more of everything—more maternity clothes and more baby accessories—than repeat mothers and parents.

Doris Fuller, of the *Los Angeles Times*, reported, "Baby-related products are proliferating." Furthermore, she quoted prospective mothers as saying, "When you're out . . . buying clothes for yourself, you feel obligated to stay in the same store" to also purchase baby items.[39] These shoppers wanted the convenience of purchasing clothes for themselves and also purchasing baby items at the same shop. Here was an opportunity for Page Boy to grab another market by expanding its merchandise and stocking baby items, but it was years before Edna Ravkind introduced high-fashion, one-of-a-kind items in her new shop, Page Boy Too, and the items Edna selected were only offered in her shop.

Swiftly changing styles favored specialty manufacturers like Page Boy and other maternity manufacturers—especially those who sold their own line of clothing—because making adjustments to their lines of clothing was easier than it was for department stores, who bought lines from manufacturers. Department stores that ordered clothes months before they expected to stock the items were not able to make changes as swiftly. This situation might have given Page Boy an opportunity to compete with the national manufacturers and chain department stores that had worked their way into its market. But two situations overshadowed the business. First Edna celebrated her seventieth birthday in 1978. It is obvious that she had caught on to Elsie's game and realized that if Elsie was shaving years from her actual age so could she. So Edna told author Lois Rich-McCoy that she was "in her 60s" when in fact she was already 71. She was still extremely active, but she was also forty years older than her customers. Elsie was nearly seventy, although she too still claimed to be much younger. Both women were active and vital, but that could not mitigate the fact that there was a great age difference between these women and their customers.

The second situation that impacted the management of Page Boy was that Elsie and Franklin Pollock had become involved not only in Beverly Hills society but also in California politics. These activities took time and distracted Elsie from Page Boy's needs.

Front cover of Page Boy catalog, 1979

Chapter 7

A Dream Fades

By the end of the 1970s, Elsie and Franklin Pollock had both run successful businesses, and now they turned their attention to conservative politics. After arriving in Los Angeles, they had been introduced to Ronald and Nancy Reagan, and Franklin even became a founding member of the Ground Floor Committee, which supported Reagan's political aspirations—especially his bid for the presidency. This association strengthened the friendship between the two men, and the Pollocks received invitations to attend the presidential inauguration and the balls celebrating Reagan's 1980 election.

Franklin and Elsie, along with many other beautiful people, flew to Washington days before the big event was to take place. All were celebrating the new administration and their own hard work that had contributed to the Republican victory. Franklin and Elsie attended the inauguration and one of the balls, and the day after the inauguration, they and a host of other supporters attended a "thank you" party hosted by President and Mrs. Reagan. The guests for this event included all those who had contributed financial support to the campaign—especially the individuals who had funded the inaugural galas. Eight hundred guests attended this event and were allowed to wander around the White House while eating and drinking. The group from California included entertainers Frank Sinatra and his wife, Barbara; Ginger Rogers; Johnny Carson and his wife, Joanna; Charleston Heston; Ed McMahon; Efrem Zimbalist, Jr.; Robert Stack and his wife; Donny and Marie Osmond; along with Franklin and Elsie Pollock. All the Hollywood guests mingled with businessmen and -women and politicians like Alfred Bloomingdale, heir to the Bloomingdale department store fortune, who was a Holmby Hills neighbor of the Pollocks; Joseph Lauder, husband of Estee Lauder; industrialist Armand Hammer; and politicians like Senator Mark Hatfield and Senator John Warner escorting his wife, Elizabeth Taylor—who could have been included in the list of entertainers with her spouse listed as senator John Warner.[1] Later that year Elsie and Franklin were invited back to the White House for a state dinner. During this event Franklin and Elsie were seated at the table with Ambassador Walter Annenberg and Art and Lois Linkletter, all acquaintances of the couple from California.

Franklin, who was in the habit of retiring for bed by ten o'clock, and who often announced to his own guests that it was time for everyone to go home, was ready to leave the festivities as his bedtime approached. That night he gathered Elsie, and they left the formal event promptly at 10:30 pm. Days later Elsie described the evening to a newspaper reporter: "There we were in the White House, in the East Room after dinner, listening to Vincent Dowling's dramatic monologue. . . . When it was over, Franklin got up and led me out to get into our car. . . . Well, next morning I found out there had been dancing after—and we'd missed it. I was furious."[2]

A few months later Nancy Reagan returned to Los Angeles to accept the American Friends of the Hebrew University of Jerusalem's 1981 Scopus Award. Included in the private reception for the First Lady were, among others, James and Gloria Stewart, Gregory Peck, Dinah Shore, Glenn and Cynthia Ford, the Ricardo Montalbans, Lucille Ball and Gary

Morton, Frank Sinatra, and Elsie and Franklin Pollock. Here was the Southern girl born in a small east Texas town, who had clawed her way up the business ladder, and now she was dining and drinking with the social and political elite. Now her name appeared in the paper not for her business acumen but for her charity work or for the position she had gained from her husband's wealth.

A few years later President Reagan appointed Elsie to serve as a board member of the National Advisory Council on Continuing Education.[3] From the newspaper accounts it is clear that Elsie had risen far from her humble roots and had entered Hollywood society. More importantly for the business, she was no longer single-mindedly focusing on Page Boy and instead was entering another world.

Despite being involved in the social life of Hollywood, Elsie continued to spend some time on Page Boy business. *Women's Wear Daily* interviewed both Edna and Elsie during March of 1984, when Elsie visited Dallas. The interview focused primarily on the history of Page Boy, but some of the information gleaned during the interview described how Edna and Elsie were managing the business—especially since one proprietor lived in Dallas, Texas, and the other in California. They told the reporter that they spoke on the phone almost daily, discussing new fashion trends, and then evaluated their marketing strategies. By this time Edna herself was managing the Galleria store in Dallas and using it as a prototype shop. She explained that in the Galleria store she even introduced "off-beat, trendier items manufactured by outside suppliers." Edna had also begun to stock nonclothing accessories, such as straw hats, shawls, and handbags, in her store. These items brought nonpregnant customers into the shop, expanding the customer base. She also changed the way the clothes were displayed and eliminated the use of mannequins in all of their stores. She converted the clothing displays to costumers, a set of hangers that could display garments and be dressed without using mannequins. Both sisters felt that mannequins became outdated too quickly and that replacing each mannequin as it became dated was a continuing expense. The change to costumers became a one-time expense, saving future expenditures. These changes and Edna's revitalization of the Galleria store made it the highest-earning Page Boy shop, based on dollars earned per square foot.

During this interview the sisters described their customers as "middle- to upper-income women in [their] late twenties to mid-30s." They continued: "If she [the customer] is not a professional, she is married to one. She is frequently well-educated, well-traveled and entertains often." Again emphasizing that Page Boy was not an innovator as far as styles were concerned, Edna said that whether the current look was "Flashdance or Victorian," Page Boy offered interpretations of the current fashions. The sisters emphasized that Page Boy also catered to the service-minded customer because it offered large, comfortable dressing rooms and well-trained staff who could match the clothes to the customers' lifestyles. In an additional endorsement for Page Boy's

ability to serve its customers, they pointed out that the firm carried maternity bras that did not look orthopedic, and they offered a "try-on" policy for maternity pantyhose—something many pregnant women requested.[4]

By the mid-1980s articles about maternity fashions often failed to include information about Page Boy styles or quotes from its owners. Nevertheless, both Elsie and Edna were still trying to keep Page Boy designs in the forefront of the maternity business. Even though Elsie was not working every day, she was still available for interviews about maternity fashion; *Los Angeles Times* columnist Jennifer Seder interviewed Elsie and several other designers and owners about the 1986 maternity fashion lines. Seder had previously written an article about maternity fashions, and although she had included illustrations of several Page Boy designs, she failed to mention Page Boy in the body of the article and had not interviewed Elsie Pollock or Edna Ravkind. In the 1986 article Seder described the mini–baby boom created by the women who were born after World War II. Explaining the rise in the number of pregnant women, designer Max DeMoss declared that it was now "fashionable to be pregnant." He explained that those women who were born between 1947 and 1960 were approaching thirty or thirty-five and were facing the end of their fertile period. Statistics indicated that the number of births was rising, and maternity clothes began to sell again. Once again, the rise brought other manufacturers into the maternity market. For example, Guess Jeans had recently opened Baby Guess boutiques, and those shops carried clothes for small children along with maternity jeans. The upscale maternity boutique Pink and Blue, located in the Los Angeles area, offered "the most expensive [maternity] items. Silk, velvet and taffeta evening gowns sell for more than $750, crepe de Chine blouses for $450." It also carried casual clothes, such as overalls trimmed with suede straps. To indulge the affluent customer, Pink and Blue added a line of fine jewelry to the other items it sold.

At about this same time Motherhood Maternity, which started in Century City, California, had accumulated 320 stores, and Mothers Work, which had started as a catalog boutique, began to open retail stores around the country. Seder noted that, during the twelve months preceding the publication of her article, seven new maternity shops had opened in the Los Angeles area alone. Phyllis Anka, sales director for Motherhood Maternity, believed that the increase in the number of outlets was stimulated primarily by the buying power of first-time mothers, especially women who were over thirty. She claimed that older women spent between $1,000 and $15,000 on their maternity wardrobes.[5] This $1,000 figure was double what had been estimated as the minimum amount that women spent a decade earlier. Again, this article failed to mention Page Boy—an indication that Page Boy was loosing out to more aggressive companies on both ends of the fashion spectrum—high-fashion maternity styles and mid- to moderately priced clothes. Fashion writers were apparently disregarding the Page Boy Company, or

Design from 1989 Page Boy catalog

they considered it insignificant or irrelevant in the overall market.

In a published interview of the next year, Sabine Brouillet, the owner of the Pink and Blue boutique in Beverly Hills, offered her formula for success. "We copy what's on the street and adapt it for maternity. That's it. It's such a simple concept, isn't it?" Brouillet added that it had taken her a long time to come up with that particular business plan. Such a statement must have been devastating to Edna and Elsie since it had been the mantra for Page Boy in 1938, 1948, and 1958. But somehow, by 1985, another firm claimed to have "found" this format and become the interpreter of current trends into maternity styles. Although Elsie had been quoted in this article, and one Page Boy dress had been illustrated with the other clothes, it was evident that other firms were now considered the leaders in maternity fashions.[6]

The next year Elsie was quoted as referring to pregnant women of the 1980s as "pregnant yuppies." She explained that these women no longer wanted suits; instead they wanted skirts and coordinating tops, rather than matching pieces. This was a look that Elsie felt was quite casual, rather than suitable for business. Gone were the days when maternity skirts and pants had stretch panels or cut outs; instead the current skirts solved the problem of the protruding abdomen with elasticized waistbands—a style that lends itself to sporty fashions but not tailored suits. Evidently, according to Elsie, even professional women no longer wore business suits or dresses. Furthermore, Page Boy had changed its manner of creating designs and formulating a seasonal line of maternity clothes, and it no longer had full-time designers on staff. Instead, the sisters hired several designers who came and went, and they even contracted for a specific number of designs. As a result, continuity and a sense of historical identity and mission were lost.

Sports outfits from Page Boy catalog, ca. 1989

During this time Page Boy introduced another way of sizing its garments. As many other firms did, Page Boy began manufacturing dresses, tops, and pants in small, medium, and large sizes. This procedure reduced the number of size gradients in which garments were made, thus reducing manufacturing costs.[7]

During the 1980s Edna, rather than Elsie, appeared more often in publicity as the face and voice of Page Boy. She even appeared as a feature personality in the "Faces" column of the *Dallas Morning News*. In this interview she reminisced about the beginning of the business, saying, "Everything I touch with my sister seems to be right." As Elsie had done for years, Edna did not include Louise's name in the Page Boy history. She continued explaining that the "new" Galleria store that had opened three years earlier was her "baby." Although it was a Page Boy shop, she said that she had introduced a line of handmade maternity clothing that included designer outfits. Perhaps Edna made these changes because she recognized the gap between what Page Boy was manufacturing and selling and what other upscale companies were offering. Or perhaps the changes Edna described in the Galleria shop represented her attempt to recapture some of the sales that the company had lost. In either case Edna's "baby" could not regain the lost share of the market alone.[8]

About this same time Edna appeared on the *Phil Donahue* show. As she had done in the December 1985 *Dallas Morning News* article, she proudly announced that she was "in charge" in Dallas and claimed that she was making decisions on her own. Finally, at the age of seventy-eight—although she also now claimed to be younger, Edna was emphasizing that the business was a partnership; she was no longer the silent partner.

Evidence suggested that, although Page Boy had lost market share to the fast growing maternity chains, it was able to maintain a sales volume that allowed it to remain profitable. In 1984 *Women's Wear Daily* reported that Page Boy owned thirty outlets. The number of outlets had been fluctuating from twenty-six to thirty during the past decade, and it is unclear whether these fluctuations represented closures and new openings or whether some numbers counted the outlet store and Page Boy Too and others did not. *Women's Wear Daily* reported that Page Boy grossed about $8 million in annual sales. These figures were a far cry from the other maternity firms and could not have funded any dynamic growth without an outside infusion of funds.[9] Moreover, when this dollar value is compared to the value of Page Boy sales during the early 1950s and adjusted for inflation, it is evident that by 1985 Page Boy's sales were roughly equal to the value of the sales it had made in 1950. It is possible that the value had increased during the intervening decades and then declined after the company discontinued wholesaling or even later in the 1980s. When these numbers are compared to those of other maternity clothing manufacturers, it is obvious that during the previous fifteen years Page Boy had been slipping behind the other chains in overall market share.

Edna and Elsie measuring a design on
a mannequin, undated

As Edna approached eighty and Elsie passed seventy-five, it became obvious that the two alone could no longer manage the firm and needed help to keep Page Boy operating and hopefully viable. Whether or not the firm could stay solvent was unclear. At the same time Franklin Pollock's son Robert had decided that he did not like practicing law and wanted to find a job in another field. To keep the control of Page Boy within the family, or perhaps to prevent the necessity of hiring an outsider, Franklin Pollock suggested that Robert Pollock move to Dallas and take over as the chief operating officer of Page Boy. Originally, he was hired in 1986 to manage the business side of the firm only, and his hiring mirrored the hiring of William Ravkind nearly twenty years earlier. He, like William, was a practicing lawyer seeking another career, not a business executive trained in either management or marketing. And, although he had grown up with Elsie running Page Boy, he had no experience in manufacturing, design, or style. Thus Pollock entered the world of women's fashion as a novice, although he had more than likely absorbed some knowledge from his stepmother.

Shortly after arriving in Dallas, Robert decided to jump in with both feet and shake up the world of maternity styles. In what was perhaps his first interview Pollock announced that Page Boy's new line would include leather miniskirts. Furthermore, he said that he had implemented a new policy for the company and that in the future the firm would only be using natural fabrics in its upcoming lines. In referring to the new styles and fabrics, he said, "You'd love to wear [them] even if you weren't pregnant. . . . You'll be astounded at the pure fashion. We have fashion and fabric contacts in New York that no one else has." Whether or not all this was true or just hyperbole is not clear; whether fabric suppliers would limit their product lines to such a small firm and whether Elsie and Edna would pay for such an extravagance if it were available are both questionable. At the same time Pollock announced that Page Boy offered a variety of design alternatives. Pollock himself favored sporty styles and touted the new line that Page Boy was manufacturing. It included a leather bomber jacket and angora-look sweaters with cowl necks.[10] Emphasizing a point that Elsie had made years earlier, he reminded customers that patterns for maternity garments were cut to fit bodies of completely different shapes than standard ready-to-wear garments. He pointed out that many of Page Boy's competitors tried to sell nonmaternity garments as maternity clothes. Finally, stressing a Page Boy essential, Pollock said that shoppers could always expect higher-quality customer service at Page Boy shops than they would receive at other stores. He reiterated that this special attention included offering busy women the opportunity to make appointments with sales staff and to have a personal shopper assist them in selecting their clothes.

Changing his focus from Page Boy's national market to the local Dallas shops, Pollock reminded the journalist that Page Boy owned shops in NorthPark, Prestonwood, and two in the Galleria. He emphasized that each of the Dallas shops was different because each reflected the individuality of the managers. And he also described Edna's shop, "Page Boy Too," as unique.[11] Such statements suggested that customers should visit all the shops because each carried distinctive merchandise.

Pollock began in the management of the company, and although he eventually worked his way

Design from 1989 Page Boy catalog

into the creative side of the business, he did modernize some of the managerial aspects of the business. Edna and Elsie had kept track of all aspects of the business with pencil and paper. Pollock, nearly two generations younger than the sisters, began to look at computers as a more modern way to keep track of production and sale. One of his most important innovations was to introduce a point-of-sale computerized inventory system in each store. Previously, sales had been reported by phone or handwritten memos that were sent to the office in Dallas, with summaries being forwarded to California. Pollock introduced computerized cash registers connected to a centralized database that automatically changed the inventory when a sale was made.

Pollack demonstrated his attraction to the fashion side of the business. "This season, Page Boy Maternity produces its most distinctive line yet. Never timid, Page Boy creates fashion for the expectant mother with the panache of an haute couture house on Seventh Avenue, announced Robert Pollock in fall of 1989." A few months later Page Boy showed a leather-and-faux–snow leopard ensemble for the holiday season. Page Boy also offered Pollock's ever favorite material—leather—in walking shorts and a long skirt. The skirt was paired with a gold lamé top. Pollock had been exposed to Elsie's penchant for international influences, and his new line included hand-embroidered and beaded tunics from India and hand-knitted, graphic-designed sweaters similar to items offered in regular ready-to-wear shops. Pollock described other offerings, such as suits in vibrant colors, as "sophisticated without the stuffiness of traditional business wear." He also brought back some couture tailoring details on many garments: pleats, tucks, buttons, gold trim, and passementerie lace.[12]

Play suits from Page Boy catalog, ca. 1989

From the very beginning Edna, Elsie, and Louise had included notes addressed to their customers in their catalogs. This system of communicating with their customers continued throughout the decades, even when Robert Pollock became COO at Page Boy. Some of the remarks printed in the brochures were short and primarily used to encourage orders. For example, in 1986 the sisters suggested that customers "shop early due to the anticipated demand" for items in the new collection. But in 1989 Edna and Elsie wrote a longer message, directly addressing career women who only had a few hours a week of "quality time." They added, "At Page Boy we can help you save some of that precious time." The letter continues by mentioning the in-house designers who "keep abreast of the European and New York Markets." The letter described how Page Boy used natural fibers; it was signed Elsie Pollock, Edna Ravkind, and "all of us at Page Boy."

The letter the next year took quite a different turn, addressing the political events that had taken place around the world. It began, "Wondrous events were transpiring in Eastern Europe while we photographed and prepared this catalog for you. The Berlin Wall was crumbling. Leaders of other Eastern Bloc Countries were driven out of office. The seeds of freedom nourished by America's shining example were taking root and blossoming." This letter continued, "We at Page Boy design and manufacture 75% of our line in our own headquarters: no one understands our vision better than we do." The letter ended by mentioning that one of the models was seven months pregnant and that Page Boy was providing "the finest maternity designs available anywhere in the world." Furthermore, Elsie and Edna dedicated the catalog to the fledgling democracies in Eastern Europe. This was a totally unique message for Page Boy but perhaps not one for some of the other manufacturers of the age, who were adding political and ecological messages to their advertisements.[13] Again this letter was signed by Elsie and Edna and "all of us at Page Boy"—but even after he had been at Page Boy nearly five years, Robert Pollack was not specifically named.[14]

Some of Robert Pollock's quotes could have come from the mouth of his stepmother, Elsie Frankfurt Pollock, back in the 1950s or 1960s. In an interview in 1991, five years after he had arrived in Texas, he said, "Forget industrial-strength classic waistlines, bows under the chin and demure floral prints," reinforcing the belief that career women needed to be seen as professionals even when they were pregnant. He continued, "A career woman in a Peter Pan collar and frilly empire waist jumper that hangs like a barrel simply won't be taken seriously . . . in court or [in] a business meeting."[15] Despite such utterances Page Boy, at least in its published brochures, did not offer business suits. The company focused primarily on sportier styles and formal dresses. Moreover, some of the designs that Robert derided were evocative of the elegant shifts worn in the 1960s, especially those styles influenced by Jacqueline Kennedy.

Pollock continued to sound much like Elsie, and

he acted as the voice of Page Boy even though Elsie and Edna were the owners. Pollock himself favored miniskirts—not really a suitable style for business settings—and his preferences influenced the Page Boy lines. He even commented that when women were pregnant they should draw attention to their legs since a pregnant woman's legs remained shapely. Using this statement as the lead-in for an advertisement, he described a new offering—a miniskirt in black-and-white polka dots with a white cotton tank top that sold for $129. Repeating his comments from an earlier interview, Pollock continued, "I am revamping the production styles." Pollock noted that his predecessors "were pushing polyester and Peter Pan collars" when he arrived, but he argued that pregnant women should avoid synthetic fibers since natural fibers breathe and keep pregnant women more comfortable.[16] He explained that he was interested in working in the maternity fashion business, saying that he had even "ditched" a law practice because none of his colleagues who were lawyers "could find sophisticated maternity styles." He portrayed himself as the "savior" of the firm, and demonstrating another lesson he had learned from Elsie, he supplied the author with a photograph of Maria Shriver wearing a Page Boy design.[17] Pollock also recommended that pregnant women should spend time focusing on themselves. Making a personal comment, he said pregnancy was "a time when men fall in love with their wives all over again."[18]

For the first few years that Pollock lived in Dallas, his name rarely appeared in local papers, but by 1991 his name began to appear often in the local *Park Cities News* and in the *Dallas Morning News.* Journalist Debrah Wormser wrote in 1991 that maternity wear was finally "growing up," implying that previous maternity fashions had not been mature or truly fashionable. As with many statements that implied that maternity fashions produced in earlier decades had not been stylish, this statement suggested that the author understood neither the vision nor Page Boy's contributions to the history of maternity wear. After all, Edna, Elsie, and Louise claimed to have accomplished this revolution in the first decades that they manufactured maternity clothes, and the sisters interpreted current fashion rather than creating a distinct line of maternity styles.

Wormser's 1991 article spotlighted two Dallas-based maternity manufacturers—Page Boy and A Pea in the Pod. A Pea in the Pod touted that it carried Victor Costa designs and owned twenty-five stores located around the country. Page Boy, by contrast, must have closed several of its shops since the article indicated that it owned only twenty-six stores in thirteen states. The article revealed that both manufacturers were emphasizing Pucci-inspired designs, but Page Boy got its due when Wormser stated that Pollock was known as the person who had introduced black leather into the wardrobe of the mother-to-be.[19]

In another interview published in the *Los Angeles Times*, Robert Pollock discussed the rising cost of maternity clothing. "You have to understand there is more fabric in a maternity garment and this costs

[more] money" than a regular garment costs, noted Pollock. He added that there was no point in Page Boy's trying to compete with the $19 maternity T-shirt offered at the Gap: since the Gap manufactured in huge quantities, it benefited from economies of scale. "They are making millions of them and we just don't have or even want that kind of cookie-cutter volume. . . . Page Boy garments are made in the United States, a more expensive undertaking than relying on import labor employed by other ready-to-wear lines." This statement makes it sound as if Page Boy still actually made high-fashion, top-of-the-line clothing; however, Page Boy was no longer competing with the high-fashion or haute couture maternity clothing lines. It had ceded the very-high-priced garments to specialty shops.[20] Page Boy's clothes were still good quality, but primarily they appealed to upper middle-class and middle-class women—not style setters.

Five years after Pollock joined the firm, he had definitely entrenched himself in the fashion side of the garment business. He said that he followed the "fashion shows in Paris and Milan" and used them as inspiration to put his stamp on the Page Boy designs. Evidently he did not believe that it was necessary to actually be at the shows and see how the garments moved on the models as Elsie had done many years earlier. Instead he relied on two-dimensional photographs and drawings. He pointed out that he controlled the style references for 1991, which paid homage to the sixties with color-block and baby-doll styles.[21] Proudly he announced that in 1991 Page Boy

Leather coat, front cover of Page Boy catalog, 1989

had only one suit in its newest line—a pantsuit that had been featured on NBC-TV's *Today* show. Reminding the author, Lisa Skolnik, that in the past celebrities often wore Page Boy clothes, he announced that Deborah Norville, Mary Alice Williams, Maria Shriver, Kim Alexis, and Jill Eikenberry had all worn Page Boy garments while being filmed for TV. He also proudly declared that Marie Osmond was a recent customer. Despite his claims to the contrary, the lack of business suits for professional women clearly indicated that the company had ceded that segment of the market to other manufacturers.[22]

When Robert Pollock arrived in Dallas, he recognized the need for change, so he tried to invigorate the firm by hiring two buyers away from A Pea in the Pod. He also began to change other aspects of the firm. He even changed the Page Boy trademark and garment tag by discarding the image of the trumpet and the page heralding the new arrival. Pollock's new trademark and garment tag evoked a more sleek, up-to-date feeling. He also changed the way the seasons' styles were planned. Page Boy designers were no longer creating related style lines based on high-fashion ideas, but instead the designers began copying from other maternity companies and designing one outfit at a time. Thus, Page Boy's mission was ignored. Not pleased with the results he obtained from hiring the new buyers and other changes he had made, Pollock fired the two buyers. Searching for another solution, he decided to hire his sister Penny.

Penny Pollock had studied fashion in Europe and was working in the garment industry in New York. Robert persuaded her to give up her New York career and to relocate in Dallas so that she could join Page Boy. After moving her family to Dallas, Penny settled in as the primary designer. Penny worked to bring new and fresh ideas to the firm, but this as-

signment was monumental, and eventually there was not enough time to start over. Page Boy's sales volume had plummeted.

As COO Robert Pollock made changes in the way that Page Boy planned out the styles for a season, and he made executive decisions about computerization and personnel. He had hired and fired lower-level employees, but Robert Pollock also took another step that directly affected his relationship with Edna. He fired longtime employee William Lackey. According to Penny, this decision was in fact made by her father, Franklin Pollock, but the physical act of firing Lackey was left to Robert. Everything about this decision was "unpleasant," wrote Penny. By this time Lackey had worked for Page Boy for at least thirty years; he had served not only as a fashion consultant with the title of vice president but as Edna's personal assistant. After the firing, Lackey was unhappy and felt that he had no one to turn to. In desperation he contacted author Lois Cowan who had previously written about the sisters under the name of Lois Rich-McCoy. Cowan had interviewed him when she was doing research about Page Boy in the mid-1970s. Cowan believes that it was Edna who fired Lackey—at least that is what Lackey told her—so Lackey never actually knew how the decision had been made. He had been astonished and angry at first and eventually totally bereft because he had dedicated himself to filling not only the business needs of Page Boy but of taking care of Edna's every whim. The firing left Lackey without a job, and Edna failed to help him find another position.[23] Lackey died in

2004, and his obituary noted that he had served as a vice president for Page Boy. He never had any real power, however, when it came to making major decisions, nor did he own a share of the firm.[24]

During the years between 1985 and 1993, many other major changes took place in the operations of Page Boy manufacturing besides the hiring of Robert Pollock. The sisters eventually decided to sell their Cedar Springs property because it was more valuable as a piece of real estate than it was as a place to manufacture their garments. This decision created a dilemma as Elsie and Edna debated about whether or not to purchase another building. Instead of buying, they decided to rent a facility. After more consideration, they decided to discontinue manufacturing their own garments, and instead Page Boy subcontracted production. That decision allowed the company to scale down its need for space. The sisters would only need to rent a location large enough to continue designing and making their samples and to contain the business office. This decision was another noteworthy shift in their business policy and was driven by two major considerations. If they were not making the clothes, they did not need to oversee workers like cutters or seamstresses, and in addition they no longer needed to worry about the rising costs of domestic manufacturing. By subcontracting the manufacturing, the company would limit its social security, liability, and health care insurance expenses. This change marked a fundamental shift in Page Boy standards.[25] Both Edna and Elsie had always insisted that Page Boy manufactured only the finest-quality clothes possible. Yet, with the manufacture of the garments now outsourced, Page Boy could no longer completely control the quality of its clothes, as it had in the past. This decline in quality control was emphasized by Brenda Berg, Louise's daughter, who explained that she noticed a marked decrease in quality between the Page Boy clothes she had worn during her first pregnancy and the clothes she wore during her last pregnancy.[26]

Page Boy's decision to contract out the manufacturing came shortly after the computer revolution hit the fashion manufacturing business. Whereas some large firms and department stores had installed computers as early as the 1960s, the computer revolution was slow to be integrated into the design and manufacturing process of upscale clothing. CAD/CAM began as a means to save cloth as the computer planned the pattern marker to minimize fabric waste. Then, by about 1990, more advanced and powerful computers were able to grade the patterns. Before this revolution it took a person about twelve hours to grade a single pattern through six sizes; in 1990 it took a computer only about two hours to do the same work.[27] These computerized systems were expensive, and when Elsie and Edna dropped wholesaling, the number of actual garments they made decreased. Thus, they could not afford a large investment in equipment because it could not be amortized across a large number of garments. The decrease in quality and the simultaneous loss of control over manufacturing directly contributed to the demise of the firm.

Despite the reduction in Page Boy's status, Page

Boy and Elsie Pollock were still important enough to be the focus of a one-page advertisement for Wausau Insurance. The advertisement, part of a thirty-six-year series based on actual firms, contains a statement that Wausau was able to consolidate all of Page Boy's insurance needs within one insurance provider and a letter to Elsie thanking her for "making our Page Boy–Wausau Story ads" and further thanking her for being such a "trouper" during the photograph session.[28]

In June of 1993, in what could be perceived as a premature memorial to Page Boy, the Dallas Jewish Historical Society sponsored a presentation titled "The History of the Dallas 'Rag Trade.'" One of the highlights of the event was a presentation by Louise Frankfurt Gartner, cofounder with her sisters of Page Boy. Gartner was the only speaker who had been an actual owner of one of the businesses featured in the presentations. The event, held at the Dallas Jewish Community Center, included presentations by Jay Lorch, the grandson of the founders of Lorch Manufacturing, and Murray and Sol Munves, representing Sunny South Fashions. The presentation also included representatives of two companies that were no longer in business, Marcy Lee Company and Nardis Company.[29]

About this same time, when Pollock had been managing Page Boy about eight years and had been acting as spokesman for several years, he finally realized that the company was continuing to fall farther and farther behind the other maternity chains in market share. Even though he had tried to shake up the company by bringing new life and new ideas into

the firm, Pollock decided his best prospect for getting some cash out of the business was to sell what was left of the firm. By this time the number of Page Boy shops had dropped to twenty-two, and those stores earned about seven million dollars in sales revenue. This figure represented a drop of a million dollars in sales revenue from the decade before. Franklin Pollock backed his son's decision, but it is not clear how thoroughly either of the men discussed the plans with either Elsie or Edna. It is clear, however, that neither man mentioned a possible sale to Penny Pollock. So, with no real attachment to the business, during the winter of 1993, Robert arranged for the sale of the Page Boy name to Mothers Work.[30]

According to Penny Pollock, both sisters were distraught at the thought of the sale. Edna took to her bed and would not comment, and Elsie became overwrought. She had always thought of Page Boy as her child. She felt trapped. She could not get angry at Robert because she knew that Franklin was behind the decision, and if she voiced her displeasure, it would only cause a row with her husband. Nevertheless, as Penny made clear, both sisters were unhappy with the decision to sell and with the price they received for Page Boy.

On January 6, 1994, Mothers Work announced that it would acquire Page Boy. The announcement said that Page Boy Maternity Co. owned twenty-two stores in fifteen states and that its sales for 1993 had been about $7 million. The day that the sale was announced, Ms. Ravkind was "unavailable for comment." Mothers Work had recently gone public, and its stock jumped from $3.25 per share before the acquisition to $16.25 per share after the purchase of Page Boy was announced. Mothers Work also announced that Robert Pollock, who was chief operating officer of the Dallas-based company would join Mothers Works as a vice president.[31]

In a subsequent article Mothers Work said the sale would close on January 31. The article indicated that most of the Dallas employees from the outlet store would transfer to one of the other Page Boy shops in Dallas so that the outlet shop could close. A few of the more senior employees would also join Pollock in Philadelphia. According to the announcement, the sale was completed to take advantage of a consolidation in the industry and to allow the "founders" to "cash out."[32]

According to the 1994 annual report of Mothers Work Inc., Page Boy had formerly been the third largest "upscale" maternity retailer in the United States. Still, as soon as Mothers Work completed the acquisition, it closed ten Page Boy stores and converted all the other stores to shops carrying names already owned by Mothers Work. Six stores reopened under the Mothers Work name itself, and six others reopened under the name Mimi Maternity, which it had previously acquired.

The 1995 Mothers Work annual report contained additional information about the Page Boy acquisition. The company reported that Page Boy had been purchased for $1 million cash and 27,438 shares of Mothers Work stock, valued at about $450,000. This valuation reflected the higher price of Mothers Work stock after the acquisition, not be-

fore. Furthermore, the report contained some accounting information that shed light on the purchase. For Mothers Work's own accounting, it allocated $818,000 to good will—an intangible asset. This accounting formula only left $182,000 as the value of Page Boy's tangible assets, such as inventory, with no liabilities. Accounting regulations changed during this time, but the decisions of allocation to tangible and intangible assets are left to the purchasing company. One wonders what Page Boy's actual value was. Mothers Work never used the name since it immediately closed the Page Boy shops, and it never marketed garments under the Page Boy name.

In the government form 10-K, filed for the year ending September 30, 1993, Mothers Work listed its assets, provided business information, and described the corporate concepts and bylaws. In a section titled "Trademarks" the company stated: "The Company owns a patent for an adjustable waistband for use in skirts which allows the garment to be loosened during the course of the pregnancy." Unlike the statement that followed, concerning the acquisition of a patent for body cream, this statement did not mention how the patent was acquired. One must assume that this statement referred to the original Page Boy patent. In a separate section the report noted that Robert E. Pollock joined Mothers Work Inc. as Vice President for Real Estate, a new position.[33] Mothers Work was creating a spot for Robert Pollock in an area in which he could hopefully excel. However, Penny Pollock, who had left a promising career as a fashion designer in New York and had come to help her brother in the family business, was not offered a position in Philadelphia.[34]

Six years later Mothers Work had gobbled up almost all the other existing maternity chains. Beginning as a catalog operation in 1982, by 1990 it had opened a few stores under the name Mimi Maternity. Mothers Work went public in 1993, the year before it purchased Page Boy. In 1995 it purchased A Pea in a Pod, the other Dallas manufacturer of maternity clothing, as well as Motherhood Maternity. As of 2000 Mothers Work operated A Pea in a Pod as an upscale chain selling clothes in the $200–$400 price range. It also operated Mimi Maternity as a distinct chain, also selling in the upscale market, with garments priced from $128 to $248. Furthermore, Mothers Work marketed clothing under two other names and was careful to locate its shops in upscale malls with anchor stores such as Nordstrom, Neiman Marcus, or Bloomingdales. That same year, it operated 672 stores and earned revenue of about $300 million. Sadly, the name Page Boy is nowhere to be found in any of the outlets.[35]

Mothers Work changed its name to Destination Maternity in December of 2008. As of 2010 it operated 1,725 retail locations, including 698 stand-alone stores and 1,027 leased departments within department stores and specialty shops. These outlets are located in all fifty states, Puerto Rico, Guam, and Canada. In 2011 Destination Maternity operated under three names: Motherhood Maternity, A Pea in a Pod, and Destination Maternity. Perhaps in an ironic twist, it no longer uses the name Mothers Work.

In analyzing the extensive accomplishments made by Page Boy and its owners, one needs to look at the situation faced by pregnant women in the late 1930s, understand how Page Boy responded to the conditions it found, and note how the situation changed over the decades. In each era the designers for Page Boy sought to design maternity outfits that mimicked the fashion trends of the time. When women wore constructed suits with nipped-in waists, Page Boy made tightly fitting skirts and sleek tops. When women wore shifts or empire designs, Page Boy manufactured similar lines. When the Edwardian look was in style, Page Boy manufactured long jackets and blouses with full sleeves. The sisters were not trying to create a new fashion trend or change the situation in which women found themselves; that was not the Page Boy mission.

Historians should not fault Edna, Elsie, and Louise for not promoting the pregnant body and pointing to the bulging abdomen. The sisters were not trying to hide or disguise the fact that women were pregnant. They simply wanted to dress pregnant women in the most appropriate way possible. Merely because they did not proclaim "Baby on Board" or design shirts that said "Baby" with an arrow pointing to the abdomen does not mean that they did not respect the pregnant woman's body. In fact, they argued that maternity designs needed to be created on a padded dress form that mimicked pregnancy, thus respecting the pregnant body's difference.

In evaluating what the Frankfurt sisters did, we

must not succumb to the process of presentism. We must not evaluate their clothes based on what is fashionable or comfortable today. To truly evaluate their accomplishments, historians must see the situation faced by pregnant women in the late 1930s, 1940s, and 1950s and understand the world not as it is now but as it was then. We must imagine ourselves working or going out in a time when all women wore slips, stockings, garter belts, heels, and often hats and gloves when they went to meetings, to play cards, to work, or to church or synagogue. The Frankfurt sisters saw this situation and responded to the need as they saw it, and their response created a successful business.

All industries are cyclical, and the fashion business is perhaps even more volatile than others due to changes in business cycles and the evolution of fashion styles. Following this economic model Page Boy had a remarkable success based on its original design of the cut-out in the skirt; then it had two more moderate innovations based on the zipper skirt and the elasticized panel hidden in the pockets. But sometime between 1960 and 1970 Page Boy lost all innovative impulses. More importantly, it succumbed to one of the major failings of family-run businesses—not planning for a future when the innovators or entrepreneurs would be unable or unwilling to run the company. Although the company remained profitable, it never went public and was undercapitalized to fund adequate modernizations or growth when competitors began to strip away its advantages. During a time of consolidation and rapid growth in the industry, Page Boy did not see the need to grow and thus lost market share to other, more aggressive firms. Page Boy made the sisters famous and wealthy, as the firm was originally organized, but it could not maintain that same business model and continue as a profitable company, nor could it expand its managerial workforce and compensate additional managers as it had the founders. Finally, the sisters made some crucial decisions, such as dropping wholesaling, that might have doomed the company years before it was eventually sold.

Neither Elsie nor Edna ever actually faced the reality that the company might have needed an extended managerial hierarchy. Even hiring Robert Pollock could not provide the necessary expertise. In evaluating the failure of another legendary Texas firm, Sanger Brothers, Leon Joseph Rosenberg wrote that "the importance of expert management cannot be overstressed." Rosenberg emphasized that companies need not a single individual (or even two, as in the case of Page Boy) but a team of individuals with specialized knowledge in specific fields who can work together to solve problems and keep a company current or modern in its operations. Rosenberg blamed Sanger's failure on the "lack of depth in management"—a problem that also plagued Page Boy.[36] It is true that Elsie had taken classes at Harvard sponsored by the Young Presidents' Organization and that she continued for several years to improve her knowledge, but between 1950 and 1980 she maintained her solo managerial style. Elsie and Edna failed to appreciate the scope of business changes that led to a revolution in manufacturing, marketing, and business management. Page Boy was born in the era when fabric was rolled out on a long table and patterns were placed on the fabric and cut by hand. It died in the era of computer-aided design, placement, and cutting. The company was born in the era of hand-operated adding machines and died in the era of computerization.

Reflecting on the names of executive that appeared in Page Boy publicity, one might assume that the company had actually expanded the number of managers taking part in business decisions. Photographs taken during a yoga break in 1963 included the comptroller, John Fulda, and the vice president and sales manager, William Moser. However, neither man was ever mentioned in later publicity, indicating that their tenure at Page Boy was limited. The 1963 financial statement, the only one available, did not mention either man. Even Abe Ravkind, Edna's husband, who was mentioned as a cutter in one article, was never listed as a manager. And while two longtime employees, William Lackey and Marjorie Rubin, remained cherished employees, they were never given true managerial responsibilities and powers. There was no ladder to climb. In the written copy for one photograph taken in California, William Lackey was identified not as a vice president but instead as a fashion advisor. He remained an employee of Page Boy and confidant of Edna Ravkind. His 2004 obituary described him as a vice president of Page Boy. But although he was a faithful employee and had some say about design choices, he had no control over actual management decisions and no ownership position.

Business historian Alfred Chandler studied both American and European firms and concluded: "Family firms were reluctant to recruit nonfamily managers and even slower to bring salaried executives into top management."[37] Although written about larger concerns in both America and abroad, this statement describes Page Boy's management policies. As the sisters aged, their unwillingness to hire any new dynamic administrators from outside the family only intensified. When they did hire family members, they never clearly defined the roles these men were to fill. That failure left the men, Ravkind and Pollock, with expectations above their actual authority. Furthermore, neither of these two men had any actual business training or fashion expertise.

When Page Boy hired William Ravkind, the sisters never gave him a contract or specified exactly what his duties or responsibilities would be. Only after Ravkind was hired and actually began working for Page Boy did he realize that he did not have the authority to make changes or to grow the company as he wanted to do in order to compete in the market of the time. He also realized that because the firm was not going to grow and expand rapidly, he would never have the ability to increase his own earning power or to own a share in the corporation, as his mother and his aunt did. Finally, Ravkind had no vested interest in the business, and he soon departed.

When Robert Pollock was hired, he did make some production and managerial changes. However, it is entirely possible that his arrival was too late to save the firm. Even his power was diminished because in the end his father wielded more power over the management of the firm, albeit covertly, than he did.

The business theories imparted by Ben Frankfurt to his daughters in the 1930s and 1940s also contributed to the downfall of the company. Frankfurt had always told his daughters not to spend money they did not have—good advice during the Depression but perhaps not good advice in the dynamic markets of the late 1950s, the 1960s, and later. In an interview early in her career, Elsie proudly declared that she had repaid the original $3,000 operating loan taken out in 1938 in less than six months. Forty years later, she said, "We never borrowed again."[38] Such principles contributed to the slow growth of the firm. Even when the company was in a very strong financial position and was the leader in maternity-fashion manufacturing, the sisters did not seize the opportunity and expand. The sisters did not take advantage of the position they had earned, and they failed to grasp the idea that growing would keep the firm from stagnating. Elsie said she wanted to grow slowly, but with the ups and downs of the maternity market and the expansion of the population, growing slowly became stagnation.

Later, when Page Boy discontinued wholesaling its garments, it lost many outlets for its brand. It is hard to determine the magnitude of this loss because no records exist indicating how many department stores had carried the Page Boy brand or what the decrease in manufactured units was. But the decrease in sales must have been significant because Page Boy was left selling its garments only in Page Boy–owned shops. In explaining the decision, Elsie said she did not want to be forced to accept returned merchandise from department stores, but sales made in department stores came without any additional costs, such as maintaining shops, hiring sales staff, or paying overhead. Reducing the number of outlets also contributed to lost sales because of the decrease in distribution, with its accompanying loss of visibility and accessibility. With fewer outlets customers needed to travel longer distances and spend more time to find Page Boy stores—something busy women could not do. Somehow Page Boy was stuck in the middle. The sisters no longer had the stamina or the will to expand the company-owned stores, and they forfeited the ability to market their brand through large department stores like many other, newer name-brand manufacturers like Liz Claiborne or even Ralph Lauren.

By the time Robert Pollock joined Page Boy, it was a dying company. Despite the fact that Pollock lacked knowledge about Page Boy's history and thus made some inaccurate statements about the firm, he made a valiant effort to revitalize the company. Pollock hired several designers and managers in an effort to reverse the decline and to improve the Page Boy lines and modernize the business operations so that Page Boy had a chance of continued success. He convinced his sister, Penny, to leave her career in the New York fashion industry to join the family firm. But still the management was filled with secrecy and confusion. Penny Pollock herself said that she would never have left her secure position in New York had she known that within a year her brother and father would be considering a merger or sale. Because they withheld the true condition of the company, she was prevented from making an informed decision about moving to Dallas. Perhaps she was not offered a position with Mothers Work because her brother was not powerful enough to negotiate a position for her when he negotiated the sale and protection for himself and a few others. But he was not trained in business or fashion and was going to Mothers Work to manage the real estate, not to continue as part of the fashion business.

This ending was a sad finish to a firm that had begun with such flair. Neither Edna nor Elsie was able to do anything to perpetuate the legacy of Page Boy or the Page Boy name. Mothers Work eventually closed the stores and never used the name, although their legal documents indicate that the name was what they purchased. In 2010, when Judie Ashworth in the publicity department of Mothers Work was contacted about locating information regarding the Page Boy acquisition, she wrote, "I have never heard about a purchase involving Page Boy."[39]

Finally, no information about Page Boy or the Frankfurt sisters could be found in the *Historical Dictionary of the Fashion Industry,* a truly sad result. These women were trailblazers in the manufacturing business and the first to manufacture fashionable maternity clothing—and they had accomplished this as women.[40]

Notes

Introduction

1. Actually there are multiple versions of how Elsie and Edna raised the funds to begin their business. One version says that they borrowed the funds from their mother without their father's knowledge. The other says that the women actually had $500 in their own savings accounts.

2. *Buttons to Biotech*. During the last half of the twentieth century, women applied for and received a larger percentage of patents than in earlier decades. By 1977 women received about 2 percent of the utility patents and about 6 percent of the design patents. By 1996 the percentages had risen to about 8-1/2 percent of utility patents and about 13 percent of design patents; email correspondence from Anne Patterson, Business librarian, Texas A&M University.

3. Blaszczyk, "Styling Synthetics." See also Economic Policy Institute information about family income.

4. Jobbers were salesmen who represented manufactur-ers and sold to small outlets or department stores. They might represent several manufacturers or only one line. After World War II many men acted as job-bers, traveling to stores in small towns. They carried samples in their cases and saved the small-town merchant the necessity of traveling to the wholesale markets.

5. See Twelfth Census, 213 B. Information provided to the author by Morris Weiss. Jenny Bergman, age 15, is enumerated with Isaac, age 40; Bessie, 35; Annie, 18; Nettie, 5; and Rosie, 4. Weiss, who has married into the family and has done some genealogical research, believes that it is possible that Bessie might not be Jenny's mother. Both Jenny and her older sister Annie were born in Russia. Moreover, there is a ten-year gap between the older two children and the younger two.

6. This story was told by both Gigi Gartner and Morris D. Weiss in emails of September 2009.

7. See Thirteenth Census, 2B.

8. "Many Buyers Come on First Day of Excursion," *Dallas Morning News*, August 18, 1909; "Big Week Expected by Dallas Jobbers," ibid., September 2, 1913, hereafter DMN.

9. Louise Frankfurt Gartner, interview by Rosalind Benjet. See Fourteenth Census. Much of the information about the family genealogy was provided to the author by Morris D. Weiss.

10. Email from Gigi Gartner, October 6, 2009.

11. A minyan is the quorum of ten adults required in Jewish law to hold public religious services. In Orthodox congregations only men or boys over the age of thirteen are counted in a minyan, but in Reform congregations that require minyans before holding services both men and women are counted.

12. Much of this information comes from the *Dallas Morning News* announcements and advertisements from late 1920s until his death in 1947. His obituary indicated that he was a retired "real estate man." DMN, December 2, 1947.

13. Texas Jewish Historical Association Archive, Apparel Manufacturing, Box 3J152.

14. Peddling was difficult in Texas because travel in undeveloped areas of the state was problematic, and most of the Jewish merchants started as small merchants or as clerks for someone else.

15. For a lengthy discussion about Jewish merchants of the nineteenth century, see Goldman, "Jewish Fringes."

16. Winegarten and Schechter, *Deep in the Heart*, 142.

17. Tolbert, *Neiman-Marcus*, 35.

18. *Handbook of Texas Online*.

19. Biderman, *They Came to Stay*, 243–44.

20. Amnéus, *Separate Sphere*, 13–55.

21. Nenadic, "Social Shaping."

22. Johnson, "Business of Fashion."

23. Amnéus, *Separate Sphere*, 13–55.

24. Peiss, "Vital Industry."

25. Smithsonian Institution Online, "First Lady of Retailing"

Chapter 1

1. This author had two great-grandmothers who worked alongside their husbands in the family's retail business, and during their last pregnancies each lost her husband. These women continued to work out of necessity. Most women who were married to merchants always worked in the family shop, even when pregnant, since it was the husbands who traveled to buy stock.

2. Poli, *Histories of Fashion*.

3. Baumgarten, "Dressing for Pregnancy."

4. Rebecca Bailey defines maternity clothing as garments designed to be worn by a pregnant woman. These garments would be fuller through the abdomen and bust and would be able to accommodate an expanding figure. Bailey, "Fashion in Pregnancy," 3.

5. Baumgarten, "Dressing for Pregnancy."

6. Troxell, *Fashion Merchandising*, 27. Upper-class women continued to have their dresses made until well into the twentieth century. Neiman Marcus was one of the first firms that specialized in high-quality garments that were not one of a kind or specially made for the customer.

7. Bailey, "Dressing for Pregnancy," 258.

8. Troxell, *Fashion Merchandising*, 26.

9. This price is low compared to the twenty-five-dollar price that Page Boy charged just two years later.

10. Lane Bryant advertisement, *New York Times*, June 1, 1937, p. 10.

11. U.S. patent number 873,167, issued to R. H. Peters, December 10, 1907.

12. Ibid. The 1910 census of Erie County, New York, listed Peters as an inventor. In the 1920 census of Monroe County and the 1930 census of Erie County, New York, he was listed as a salesman.

13. U.S. patent number 960,689, issued to William Padernacht, December 10, 1907.

14. U.S. patent number 1,172,102, issued to G. Baer.

15. U.S. patent number 1,357,828, issued to C. M. Goldberg; U.S. patent number 1,333,410, issued to W. Gerber; U.S. patent number 2,051,444, issued August 18, 1935; and U.S. patent number 2,085,179, issued June 29, 1937. This is not an all-inclusive list of patents issued during the first half of the twentieth century for maternity garments.

16. Troxell, *Fashion Merchandising*, 26.

17. Edna Frankfurt Ravkind had a history of taking risks on business ventures. In fact, in 1935 she and her parents invested $3,000 to establish Frankfurt, Ravkind Inc., a Dallas merchandising firm. The charter was relinquished in 1950. DMN, May 16, 1935; State of Texas corporate records.

18. DeMoss, *Apparel Manufacturing in Texas*, 44.

19. The published stories recount that the incident took place in 1937 or 1938. However, Elsie graduated from Southern Methodist University in June of 1934. Thus, she had been out of college for three or four years when the incident took place. This claim illustrates Elsie's fondness for altering facts, especially dates, to suit her purposes—by making stories more exciting or herself younger. DMN, June 5, 1934.

20. Worden, "Maternity Can Be Chic," 26–27.

21. As with other parts of the story of how Page Boy came into being, this may not be exactly how things happened; the first advertisement appeared in the *Dallas Morning News* in December of 1937. Moreover, the sisters did not apply for a patent until June 3, 1938, not the same summer Elsie imagined the design. Thus, Page Boy possibly had a slightly slower beginning than Elsie claimed. Also, in stories about the opening of the shop, if Elsie moved the date a year or two later, she could easily claim to be younger than she actually was—something she asserted throughout her later life. In *Millionairess* by Rich-McCoy, Elsie says that Edna was twenty-three when they made the first suit. But Edna would have been nearly thirty. I believe that both women whittled years off their ages. This reduction was possible since Edna was born in 1908 and Elsie in 1911, but Louise was not born until 1921. Thus, each could move her age closer to that of Louise without causing much tumult in the family. Ill-fitting maternity garments continued to cause problems throughout the twentieth century and even into the twenty-first century. As dresses got shorter and less bulky, the skirts hiked up over the abdomen. This especially became a problem as skirts were cut to fit tightly around the waist and hips with very little extra width around the hem. This was the problem that Elsie Frankfurt faced in 1937, and although the problem was solved temporarily by Elsie's inventive talent, other designers continued to seek alternative designs to solve the problems. Elsie's design solution fit the styles of the age, the 1930s, 1940s, and early 1950s. But changes in fashion drove the creative impulse, and many other designers applied for and received patents for maternity garments. For example, in 1959 Lucille McMann also patented a design with a narrow silhouette. Her idea built

on Elsie's design, but instead of having a skirt with an opening in the front, she designed a dress made of a skirt and bodice sewn together with an oval opening that began under the bust and extended to below the waist. The dress was worn with a top made of the skirt fabric. This gave the appearance of a suit. This patent was issued in September of 1962. Four years later a patent for a skirt with removable elasticized panels was issued. This patent did not have an accompanying top or blouse. In February of 1974, Gloria Kadison received a patent for an adjustable skirt. By the 1980s fabrics had evolved, and many stretchable fabrics had come into the market. In addition, the styles had changed. Stiffly constructed suits with tight-fitting skirts were no longer in fashion. In response to changes in style, Marilyn Stern received a patent for a skirt that could be worn both during pregnancy and after. It had a very wide expandable waistband made of gathered fabric that could be let out or taken in. In 1999 Vivian Blair received a patent that allowed a pregnant woman to continue wearing her button-up jeans. The patent was for a V-shaped insert with buttonholes on one side and buttons on the other. The woman could button the panel onto her own jeans by buttoning the panel onto the button holes of her garment, then buttoning the buttons of the garment through the buttonholes on the panel. Innovation never stops, and inventors received two patents for maternity garments in 2009.

22. According to an interview conducted in 2006 with Louise Frankfurt Gartner, one of her sisters—most likely Elsie—owned a small dress shop in the Medical Arts Building before she started manufacturing maternity clothes. Because she realized that many of the women who regularly passed by her shop needed maternity clothes, she decided that making fashionable maternity outfits could lead to a business success. In this interview Louise also mentioned that even while she was in high school she had helped in the business by going to the wholesale market and selecting styles for the shop. Louise Frankfurt Gartner, interview by Rosalind Benjet.

23. "New Page Boy Store Shows Page Boy Dresses," DMN, December 5, 1937.

24. In some stories the opening date is as late as 1939. For various stories covering the beginning of Page Boy, see Worden, "Maternity Can Be Chic"; "Maternity-Dress Millions"; "Enterprising Team," *Dallas Morning News*, September 4, 1949; and Galonoy, "Isis of Texas," pp. 10–13, 45.

25. Patent available at http:patft.uspto.gov.

26. Elizabeth King Scott, "Flowers on Your Wardrobe," DMN, April 24, 1938.

27. Rich-McCoy, *Millionairess*, 98–99. This indicates that the sisters averaged about $500 profit each month during their first six months of business. (Rich-McCoy now writes under the name Lois Cowan.)

28. *Collier's,* March 1950. In this article Elsie claimed that she was twenty-one when she went to New York, but the trip occurred in 1939 or 1940 and she was already twenty-eight or twenty-nine.

29. "How She Made a Million," newspaper article dated March 3, 1958, Page Boy scrapbook.

30. Worden, "Maternity Can Be Chic"; DeMoss, *Apparel Manufacturing in Texas*, 45.

31. Sylvia Weaver, Adjustable Skirt Solves Blessed Event Problem," *Los Angeles Times*, May 9, 1939.

32. *New York Times*, October 10, 1939.

33. *Atlanta Constitution*, October 11, 1939.

34. Scott, "Flowers on Your Wardrobe," DMN, April 24, 1938.
35. DMN, March 23, 1938.
36. Phone interview, Rosalie Ravkind, April 30, 2010.

Chapter 2

1. This is west of downtown Los Angeles and east of the current shopping mecca of Rodeo Drive.
2. Gigi Gartner, email to author, October 7, 2009.
3. *Los Angeles Times*, September 18, 1940. Beginning in 1940 and continuing through the 1960s, Page Boy ran regular advertisements in the *Los Angeles Times*.
4. *Collier's*, March 25, 1950. Sullivan was the first of many movie and TV stars to patronize Page Boy. Margaret Sullivan was an American film and stage actress who was once married to Henry Fonda. She was married three more times.
5. See, e.g., DMN, May 10, 1941.
6. Louise Frankfurt Gartner, owner of Page Boy, interview by author, July 26, 2008; "Enterprising Team," DMN, August 4, 1949.
7. Jane Guzman, email of March 26, 2010. Twenty-four years later Jane also purchased samples from the Dallas outlet. Purchasing Page Boy clothes became a family tradition for many women in the Dallas Jewish community.
8. Ray W. Bonta, "Business News Notes," DMN, March 3, 1943. Information about the film and stills is in the Margaret Herrick Library, Beverly Hills, California. It was a black-and-white film released on February 28, 1942, with a running time of ten minutes. The credits are as follows: producer and narrator, Pete Smith; director, Will Jason; original story and screenplay, Joe Ansen; film editor, Philip Anderson; sound, Western Electric; cast, Dave O'Brien, Mary Shepherd. Synopsis: Pete Smith takes a look at a young couple expecting their first child. The husband, on reading a pamphlet stating that he should "humor her little whims," is exhausted by the time baby arrives.
9. *Los Angeles Times*, May 26, 1941, June 9, 1941, August 3, 1942, and August 14, 1942.
10. Joan Susman, email to author, April 19, 2010.
11. DMN, March 23, 1941. Additionally, Edna's Social Security card was issued to her while she lived in California, adding credibility to the fact that at least for a time she resided in the Los Angeles area. See Ancestry Library, Edna Ravkind death index, http://search.ancestrylibrary.com/. Edna's actions were not unusual. Many family members living away from home returned to be near parents or siblings when the war broke out.
12. Heath, "American War Mobilization."
13. Ibid.
14. DeMoss, *Apparel Manufacturing in Texas*; *Handbook of Texas Online*, s.v. Clothing Manufacturing.
15. "Wholesalers Told to Face Sacrifices," DMN, December 9, 1942.
16. During midcentury fashions changed rapidly. Each season dramatic changes took place in women's fashions. One season skirts might be short, and the next season they would be five or six inches longer; full skirts might be all the rage one year, and then no one wore that style the next year. Colors were also considered a fashion statement. One fall the "new" color might be burgundy, and the next season it would be burnt orange. During the war the focus was on stability in styles so that women would not consider an outfit out of style simply because it was two years old.
17. Nolan, "Women's Fashion History."

18. My mother was born in 1917, and she spoke of knowing most of the other people born about that time, including Stanley Marcus and the Frankfurt sisters. Leslie Wagner, archivist for the Dallas Jewish Archive, confirmed that until about the middle of the century the Dallas Jewish community was quite cohesive and most Jews knew other members of the community (email of August 6, 2010). Lester Lorch was born in 1902 and Stanley Marcus in 1905, making them about the same age as Edna Frankfurt, who was born in 1908. Author Rose Biderman estimated that the Dallas Jewish population was about 10,000 in 1940.

19. "Women Take Clothing Restrictions Cheerfully," DMN, May 25, 1943.

20. Rich-McCoy, *Millionairess*, 101.

21. Ralph Zeman, former garment manufacturer from Dallas, interview by author. Although Zeman did not specifically say who offered additional fabric for money, he indicated that it was either the fabric manufacturers or suppliers.

22. *Los Angeles Times*, August 14, 1942.

23. According to Ralph Zeman, cutters were always men.

24. DMN, August 8, 1943.

25. DMN, January 2, 1944.

26. Barbara Bundschu, *Binghamton Press*, March 5, 1947.

27. DMN, June 21, 1944.

28. After the war, all the Dallas-based companies grew rapidly, but according to the *Dallas Morning News*, Page Boy's growth was even more phenomenal than that of the other firms. However, its growth was obscured in figures referring to the overall expansion.

29. "Dallas Praised for Its Style," DMN, May 10, 1944; "Fashion Art," DMN, May 11, 1944,

30. DeMoss, *Apparel Manufacturing in Texas*, 43.

31. Ibid., 44.

32. "Dallas-Born Idea Grows into National Business," *Dallas Times Herald*, November 20, 1946.

33. "Deaccentuating the Positive," DMN, December 22, 1946, section 5 p 1. In this article Elsie is reported to be thirty and Louise twenty-five. This is incorrect since there is a ten-year difference between their ages, and Elsie was born in 1911. This continues the pattern of Elsie asserting that she was younger than she actually was.

34. Gay Simpson, :Fashion Perplexities Are Solved," DMN, July 13, 1947.

35. *Collier's*, March 25, 1950.

36. Alice Hughes, "New York Report," *Times Herald*, February 22, 1947; "The March of Industry," a pamphlet from the Page Boy collection; Rich-McCoy, *Millionairess*, 103. The version in Rich-McCoy's book varies somewhat from the others.

37. "Engagement Announced, "DMN, April 13 1947 and Ben Frankfurt December 2, 1947.

38. "Two New Birds for the Zoo," DMN, August 11, 1949.

39. "Battle of the Bulge," *Time*, September 6, 1948.

40. "Page Boy Trademark Known Coast to Coast," DMN, June 5, 1949.

41. This corner of Cedar Springs and Olive Street is near downtown Dallas, just north of Woodall Rogers Freeway.

42. Brenda Berg, telephone interview by author, April 14, 2010. As an adult remembering through a child's eye, Brenda believes that the cleanliness, décor, and brightness of the offices and manufacturing areas made Page Boy a "good place to work." By comparison, this author can remember visiting her uncle's factory, which was located in downtown Dallas. That factory was dark

and musty; the huge room had small windows along the walls with cutting tables in one area and sewing machines in another.

43. The fact that Page Boy included a workers' exercise room in its building built in 1949 indicates that even at this time, before they became involved in yoga, the owners were interested in the health and wellbeing of their workers.

44. Newspaper article from Page Boy scrapbooks belonging to Elsie Frankfurt.

45. *New York Times*, August 31, 1949.

46. Louise Frankfurt Gartner, interview by Rosalind Benjet.

47. "Enterprising Team," DMN, August 4, 1949.

48. "Business Students at SMU to Observe Anniversary," DMN, May 7, 1950.

Chapter 3

1. In January of 1950, the sisters closed the shop in the Medical Arts Building but opened another shop at 110 South Ervay Street in Dallas. DMN, January, 22, 1950.

2. *Wall Street Journal*, September 6, 1949.

3. *Los Angeles Times*, various advertisements throughout 1950 and 1951.

4. *Independent*, Pasadena, California, May 21, 1956, from the Page Boy collection; Katherine Dillard, "The Woman's Angle," DMN, August 9, 1951. Two decades later the dolls were donated to the Dallas Museum of Fashion, which was housed in the Texas Fashion Collection at North Texas State University in Denton.

5. Currently the dolls and their traveling trunks are housed in the Fashion Collection of the University of North Texas. Edward Hoyenski, the collection manager, has been working to repair the broken dolls; he

believes that the dolls were miniature mannequins and most likely made for Page Boy by a mannequin manufacturing company. There are no marks on the dolls indicating who made them.

6. Leonard Lyons, *San Mateo Times*, September 6, 1948, and *Washington Post*, August 31, 1948.

7. *Los Angeles Times*, July 2, 1951.

8. "When a Designer Has a Baby," *Good Housekeeping*, July 1951: 78–80.

9. "The Signal," Winter 1954, from Page Boy scrapbook. This is the only time that the names of other designers were mentioned in print.

10. DMN business section, August 25, 1951.

11. This story, written by syndicated columnist Phyllis Battles and Dorothy Roe, Associated Press women's editor, was reported in multiple articles appearing from September 30 through October 7, 1951. Although Elsie was actually older than the age limits, more than likely the current members were too chivalrous to ask for her birth certificate, and she continued to subtract years from her age.

12. DMN business section, August 25, 1951.

13. "Wardrobe for Actor's Wife," DMN, September 2, 1953.

14. According to Penny Pollock, Elsie believed that she should never pay for advertisements, especially since she had always gotten so much publicity without paying.

15. "Elsie Frankfurt Receives 1951 *Mademoiselle* Award," DMN, December 17, 1951. Elsie continued to promote her self as younger than she actually was, and the press release for the award stated that all the winners were between the ages of seventeen and thirty-two.

16. Dorothy Roe, *Chester* (PA) *News*, April 15, 1951.

17. DMN, March 3, 1951.

18. Barbara Brady, "As Elastic as Waistbands," DMN, January 3, 1952.

19. Page Boy catalog, Fall/Winter 1952, from Page Boy scrapbook.

20. Page Boy catalog, Fall/Winter 1952, inside back cover.

21. *Los Angeles Times*, Display Advertisement, January 20,1952

22. Fay Hammond, *Los Angeles Times*, May 7, 1952.

23. Page Boy advertising booklet, Spring/Summer 1953, and Page Boy advertising booklet, Fall/Winter 1953, in Page Boy collection in the Texas Fashion Collection.

24. K. Dillard, "County's Apparel Industry Shows Tremendous Growth," DMN, January 18, 1953.

25. For information about women in the workforce during the 1950s, see Meyerowitz, "Beyond the Feminine Mystique" and Weiner, *From Working Girl*.

26. Zeman, interview by the author, July 25, 2008, and Gartner, interview by the author, July 26, 2008.

27. "NLRB Dismisses Union Complaints," DMN, November 24, 1953. The union also claimed that Edna Frankfurt Ravkind's husband, Abe, was listed as a cutter—a laborer. Such a relationship caused technical problems with the union because owners were considered as managers and cutters were considered as laborers. Union regulations prevented a worker from also being a manager, and Abe's relationship to the managers (i.e., his wife) was questioned.

28. Clavert, De León, and Cantrell, *History of Texas*, 358; Handbook of Texas Online s.v. International Ladies' Garment Workers' Union.

29. Eleanor Roberts, "Petticoat President," *Boston Post*, January 28, 1954.

30. Email exchange between Joan Susman and author, October 2009.

31. Brenda Berg, telephone interview by the author, April 14, 2010.

32. *Los Angeles Times* and *Dallas Morning News* advertisements, July 17 and 18, 1955.

33. Elsie Frankfurt, DMN, July 28 through August 7, 1956.

34. Eleanor Roberts, "Dainty Texas Tycoon Is Queen for a Week at Harvard Seminar," *Boston Post*, February 7, 1956.

35. Marjorie Farnsworth, "Woman of the Week," *Journal American*, February 25, 1956, from Page Boy scrapbook.

36. *Los Angeles Times*, May 13, 1956.

37. *Gazette*, Charleston, West Virginia, July 9, 1956.

38. Clippings dated June 27, 1956, from Page Boy scrapbook.

39. *Washington Post* and *Times Herald*, January 27, 1957.

40. Galanoy, "Isis of Texas," *Empire for Young Executives*, 1959 Frankfurt folder box 97–003/46, Steve Carlin Papers.

41. *Los Angeles Times*, February 17, 1957.

42. Garroway was the first host of NBC's *Today* show, the national morning television show.

43. Gay Simpson, "Stars Bank of Fashion by Page Boy," DMN, November 5, 1957.

44. DMN, September 22, 1957.

45. Virginia McCallon, "New Trends Are Adopted for Maternity Designs, *Houston Post*, February 6, 1959.

46. This fact was exemplified in reverse as Edward Hoyensky, manager of the fashion collection at the University of North Texas, explained: when he began photographing the Page Boy outfits that the university owned, he and the photographer realized that the dresses did not look good on a regular mannequin and that they needed to pad the form to appear pregnant. Only after they did this did the dresses regain a stylish look.

47. *Dallas Times Herald*, November 20, 1957. This statement, along with the fact that Louise got less and less publicity as the decade progresses, suggests that perhaps a rift was forming between the sisters. Although Louise denied that there was any tension, Edna's daughter acknowledged that there was friction between Edna and Elsie in later years. Additionally, it was evident from my interviews that the sisters did not maintain contact after the business was sold. In fact, one daughter mentioned that the family had never been close, adding that they did not celebrate holidays together like many Jewish families do.

48. DMN, September 29, 1956. Other designers listed Page Boy on their resumes, but Elsie never mentioned that anyone other than she and Louise designed clothes.

49. *Gettysburg Times*, July 30, 1958.

50. *All Florida Weekly Magazine*, March 9, 1959.

51. Rosalie Ravkind, Edna Frankfurt's former daughter-in-law, telephone interview by author, April 30, 2010.

52. Ruth Wagner, "Page Boy Fashion Designer," *Washington Post*, January 29, 1958.

53. Berta Mohr, "Slim Look Achieved by New Styling, *Stanford Connecticut Advocate*, February 10, 1958.

54. DMN, April 4, 1958.

55. Babette, *Los Angeles Examiner*, May 19, 1958, and *Women's Wear Daily*, May 20, 1958.

56. *Women's Wear Daily*, July 22, 1958.

57. This shop was not connected with the Casual Corner chain.

58. *Women's Wear Daily*, May 20, 1958.

Chapter 4

1. All of Edna's dance costumes were created in the factory. She herself favored less flashy fashion-forward clothing; however, her dance costumes were just the opposite. On the dance floor she wore full flowing skirts filled with sequins, and often her skirts were trimmed with fur or feathers. Brenda Berg, telephone interview by the author, April 14, 2010.

2. "The Jackie Influence," DMN, May 2, 1963. Between 1959 and 1963 the three Kennedy wives gave birth to six children, so they were often seen in maternity clothes.

3. Acquisition data sheet, Texas Fashion Collection.

4. Gay Pauley, *Chicago Tribune*, April 28, 1963.

5. Anne Yates Clarke, "Jackie Excites Maternity Wear Makers," *New York World-Telegram*, April 17, 1963.

6. Fairfax Nisbet, "Theater-of-the Air," DMN, February 3, 1960.

7. DMN, November 27, 1957.

8. "Theater-of-the Air," DMN, June 12, 1963.

9. Joan McKinney, "What Happened to the Stage Door Johnnies?" *San Francisco Chronicle*, July 16, 1961.

10. Frogs are ornamental closures usually made of braid or cord. They are often found on Asian-inspired garments.

11. Helanca was an early, sturdy, stretch fabric.

12. *The Plain Dealer*, August 11, 1963, and DMN, August 6, 1963.

13. Kermit Jaediker, *Daily News*, November 16, 1963. In the interview for this article, Elsie said they had one customer who arrived at the shop looking for a dress to wear at her wedding. Since the company did not make wedding dresses, Page Boy custom made her a dress that she could wear, and no one knew that she was four months pregnant. Information about this style show was also found in articles from the *Chicago Daily*

News, Lacona (NY) *Citizen, Amarillo Globe, Lima* (Ohio) *Citizen,* and other newspaper articles found in the Page Boy scrapbooks.

14. Frances Borzelle, *Chicago Tribune,* July 23, 1963. I was pregnant in 1963–64, and although I made many of my own dresses, I did purchase several dresses in the ladies' ready-to-wear department rather than the maternity department.

15. Rosalie Ravkind, interview by the author, April 30, 2010. Darin and Dee visited Dallas in August and September of 1961. See DMN.

16. This skirt design resembles men's golf slacks that have elastic hidden beneath the pocket. These elastic insets stretch and provide several additional inches of room around the waist, but the elastic is never seen because the expansion is hidden under the pocket.

17. Jane Guzman, like her mother, wore Page Boy sample designs that were purchased at the office, not the outlets; according to her, this new fabric was similar to thick cotton knit. Guzman, conversation with the author, April 2, 2010.

18. This columnist used only one name in her byline.

19. Late in November of 1963, excitement spread through Dallas and especially Page Boy's factory. President Kennedy was coming to Dallas on his trip through Texas. Before he arrived, his office announced that his motorcade would travel down Cedar Springs en route from Love Field to downtown Dallas. Everyone at the plant enthusiastically made plans to be on hand that morning. Elsie brought her children to the factory so that they could share in the historical event. As his arrival time neared, all the employees and the family members who had joined in the festivities that morning lined up on the sidewalk, waiting for the president and his motorcade to pass by. After the motorcade passed the corner, all the workers and family members returned to work. Within a short time they heard the horrifying news that the president had been killed. Brenda Berg, telephone interview by the author, April 14, 2010.

20. Ruth Wagner, *Washington Post,* March 31, 1962; *Christian Science Monitor,* May 14, 1962; and other articles dated April 1962 from *Chicago Daily Tribune, Dallas Morning News,* and *Los Angeles Times.*

21. Jane Guzman, native of Dallas and Page Boy patron, telephone interview by the author, April 2, 2010.

22. Carl W. Ritter, "Texas Gals Tops in Their Field," *San Diego Union,* August 30, 1963.

23. Fred Rothenberg, "Pauley Thrives with Job and Family," *Los Angeles Times,* July 22, 1986.

24. Although Elsie later claimed credit for bringing yoga to the firm, Louise said that she was the sister who introduced yoga to her sisters and later wanted to introduce it at the factory.

25. Devi, *Renew Your Life,* 93–98.

26. Kermit Jaediker, *New York Daily News,* November 15, 1963.

27. Devi, *Renew Your Life,* 93–98. Devi was born in Latvia and escaped from Moscow barely ahead of the Communist revolutionaries. She moved from Europe to India when she was about twenty-seven and took an Indian name.

28. "Yoga Authority Influences Maternity Fashion," DMN, October 20, 1963.

29. "Yoga Break," DMN, October 22, 1963.

30. "Yoga Authority Influences Maternity Fashion," DMN, October 20, 1963.

31. Kermit Jaediker, *Daily News,* November 15, 1963.

32. *Life* 56, no. 7, 97.

33. Arlene Dahl, "Let's Be Beautiful," *Chicago Tribune,* April 24, 1964.

34. David R. Brown, "Sweating it Out: Desk Bound Executives Decide That Exercise Is Worth the Effort," *Wall Street Journal*, May 2, 1968.

35. Extensive searches in business, yoga, and social science journals revealed few references to exercise or yoga in the workplace prior to 1980 when exercise and relaxation therapy was promoted for individuals but not usually in the workplace.

36. Pam DeCastro, "Bay State Companies Are Encouraging Wellness," *Boston Business Journal*, March 24, 1986: 22–23.

37. *Western Apparel*, October 1962.

38. *New Yorker*, November 18, 1961.

39. *Ebony*, February 1963: 111–14.

40. Walker, *Women's Magazines*, 7.

Chapter 5

1. *Newsday*, February 14, 1958.

2. During the 1960s some states limited the number of hours and times of day that women could work. For example, women might not be allowed to work after 6:00 p.m. or earlier than 8:00 a.m. The rationalization for such laws was that they protected women from being out alone late at night.

3. Pat Herman, "American Women Are Second-Class Citizens! Feminine Wrath Is Rising against Laws That Penalize Women under the Guise of Protecting Them," *Family Weekly*, April 12, 1964. *Family Weekly* was a newspaper supplement that was carried in more than 350 newspapers. Married Texas women suffered under multiple disabilities until 1972 when an equal rights law was passed. For example, until that time, a married woman could not purchase an automobile in her own name, even if she was using her own money, unless she obtained her husband's permission.

4. Steve Carlin Papers, Box 97–003/46.

5. "Land Deal Closed for $1,500,000," DMN, December 6, 1963. NorthPark Shopping center opened in August of 1965. The location is approximately where Coffee Park is currently located.

6. Ruth Wagner, "Page Boy's Elsie Frankfurt: Texas Tycoon Takes Time for Small Business Junket," *Washington Post*, June 22, 1964; DMN, June 6, 1964; and Marilyn Bender, "Maternity Manufacturer Is a 'Hit' on Tunisian Trip," *New York Times*, June 29, 1964. It is interesting to note that this last article began with the words, "A spinster maternity magnate." So, even in 1964 and when she was serving in a public capacity, Elsie was still identified as a "spinster."

7. Eugene P. Foley letter from Page Boy scrapbook.

8. Marylin Bender, *New York* Times, May 2, 1964.

9. Almost all written accounts that mention Lotus indicate that Elsie was the owner and motivation behind the company. In one interview with Martin Abramson, however, Elsie said that Lotus was a subsidiary of Page Boy. In this interview Elsie also said that she and her sisters had invested in suburban shopping malls in Dallas, Houston, and New Orleans.

10. Elsie Frankfurt, DMN, March 3–April 4, 1964.

11. "World's Fair Dress," DMN, May 6, 1964. About this time nylon invisible zippers began to be used in dresses and other garments. The switch from metal to nylon decreased the heft of the garment, which meant that zippers could be added as a design element without weighing down the garment.

12. Gay Simpson, DMN, February 16, 1964.

13. Prior to 1980 camisoles were short undergarments worn over a brassiere and under a blouse. They stopped a few inches below the waist and could be worn under sheer blouses that were worn with slacks or lined skirts.

14. "On and Off the Avenue: This and That," *New Yorker*, May 1, 1965.

15. *Scottsdale Daily Progress*, January 10, 1966.

16. It was not clear where the Lotus dresses were manufactured. If they were made at the Page Boy factory, that situation raises questions about who actually owned Lotus. If Elsie owned it, did Lotus pay Page Boy for the use of Page Boy's facilities? Or was the line owned by both Edna and Elsie with Edna serving as a silent partner? These are questions that can only be solved by finding business documents.

17. *New York Times*, January 24, 1965; see Media Storehouse, http://www.mediastorehouse.com/pictures_618148/REAGAN-CHESTERFIELD-AD.

18. "Page Boy Keynotes Elegance in Styling," DMN, August 19, 1965.

19. Brenda Berg, telephone interview with the author, April 14, 2010.

20. Louise Gartner, interview with the author, July 26, 2008, Dallas, Texas.

21. Kent Biffle, "Envoy Tells of Tunisia's Great Society," DMN, June 21, 1966.

22. Martin Abramson, "The New Look in Lady Millionaires," *Good Housekeeping*, September 1967. Elsie looked so youthful that she could claim to be in her mid-forties when in fact she was actually fifty-six at the time the article was published.

23. L. Gross, "Self-Made Woman," *Look*, February 14, 1961.

24. Joan Susman, email to the author, April 19, 2010.

25. L. Gross, "Self-Made Woman," *Look*, February 14, 1961. The irony of her words must have hit columnist Jack O'Brian because the week after the story appeared in *Good Housekeeping*, he mentioned that the magazine had a "fine piece on self-made millionaire Elsie Frankfurt," adding "bachelorette." Jack O'Brian, "Voice of Broadway," *Palladium Times*, Oswego, New York, October 7, 1967.

26. "Seen Thru the Looking Glass: Another Bride in her Bridal Gown," *Chicago Tribune*, August 8, 1966.

27. Rich-McCoy, *Millionairess*, 106–8. Rich-McCoy, now Lois Cowan, says that Elsie never ran a D & B on Pollock, but the family says that each ran one on the other and later laughed about it.

28. Martin Abramson for Feature Syndicate, May 3, 1968.

29. Karol Stonger, DMN, August 6, 1967.

30. Rosalie Ravkind, interview with the author, April 30, 2010.

Chapter 6

1. Because there are so few business papers, it is not clear whether Louise ever actually owned a share of the business or whether her involvement was based on some other arrangement.

2. Louise Frankfurt Gartner, interview with the author, July 26, 2008.

3. For example, this author has spoken to many Texas women who are currently in their sixties whose mothers took them to purchase Page Boy clothes when the daughters became pregnant. The mothers remembered that Page Boy clothes had been the most fashionable and stylish maternity clothes they had worn, and they wanted to outfit their daughters in a similar way.

4. Although oral contraceptives had been on the market

for some medical problems, they were not universally available to all women across the United States until after *Griswold v. Connecticut* in 1965. This case, which went to the U.S. Supreme Court, made oral contraceptives generally available to married women but not single women.

5. One way to gauge the change in attitude toward number over quality is to examine the size of the closets built in houses constructed in the 1940s and 1950s, compared to those in houses built in the 1980s and later.

6. Walker, *Women's Magazines*, 207.

7. Patricia Shelton, *Christian Science Monitor*, October 4, 1968; "Odds Look Good in the Waiting Game," DMN, September 8, 1968.

8. Richard Baskin, "Centers Cater to Mothers-To-Be," *Christian Science Monitor*, January 12, 1971.

9. DMN, July 9, 1967.

10. DMN, February 20, 1968.

11. Several family members reported that Page Boy was Elsie's baby, and like a mother she never wanted to relinquish supervision of her child to someone else.

12. Undated booklet from Page Boy scrapbook. This book was probably published around 1970 or 1971.

13. Brenda Berg, interview by the author, April 14, 2010.

14. Mitchell and Sklare, *Mishpokhe*, 39–41.

15. Forming family clubs or family circles was not an unusual practice among Eastern European Jewish families.

16. Joan Susman, email to the author, April 19, 2010.

17. Penny Pollock, interview with the author, September 29, 2009.

18. Jody Jacobs, "Sunday Night Supper Parties Are Here to Stay," *Los Angeles Times*, February 16, 1975.

19. Jody Jacobs, "State Chili Champ to Defend Title," *Los Angeles Times*, May 2, 1976; "Sunday Night Supper Parties are Here to Stay." *Los Angeles Times*, February 16, 1975.

20. Penny Pollock, interview with the author, September 29, 2009.

21. "Page Boy Shop Shows Collection for Holidays," *Los Angeles Times*, December 14, 1972, and "Page Boy Makes Stylish Maternity Fashions," DMN, August 11, 1972.

22. Rich-McCoy, *Millionairess*, 117–21.

23. Ibid.

24. Penny Pollock, interview with the author, September 29, 2009.

25. Harry Bowman, DMN, May 9, 1974; *Los Angeles Times*, May 6, 1974.

26. Unidentified newspapers dated March 22 and March 30, 1973, from Page Boy scrapbook.

27. Pat Kivesty, "Page Boy Maternity: The Ladies and the Label," *WWD*, March 20, 1984. It is possible that if Edna and Elsie had hired a manager from outside the family, they could have continued to sell wholesale. Other firms made money wholesaling, and perhaps this is an example of age catching up with Edna and Elsie. They could not manage all the divisions of the company themselves and were unwilling to bring in an outside manager.

28. "New Page Boy Fashions Unveiled," *Los Angeles Times*, September 26, 1974; *Acadia* (California) *Tribune*, November 28, 1974.

29. "Firm Adopts Own Slogan," DMN, March 16, 1975. This article mentions that Edna was now the executive head of the firm and the only one of the sisters who was still active in the business.

30. *Los Angeles Times*, November 7, 1976.

31. "On Fashion," *Los Angeles Times*, July 18, 1977.

32. *Dallas Times Herald*, January 10, 1979.

33. Earl Gottschalk Jr. "Sales of Maternity Clothes Are Booming, Fueled by Working-Women Pregnancies," *The Wall Street Journal*, July 14, 1980.

34. "The Svelte Look: Rebirth for Maternity Retailing," *Business Week*, December 18, 1978, 100–103.

35. Ibid.

36. Marylou Luther, "Clotheslines," *Los Angeles Times*, October 31, 1976, and February 16, 1979.

37. Earl Gottschalk, Jr., "Sales of Maternity Clothes Are Booming, Fueled by Working-Women Pregnancies," *Wall Street Journal*, July 14, 1980.

38. Claudia Ricci, "Now for the Expectant Executive: Women's Suits With a Fuller Cut," *Wall Street Journal*, February 11, 1983. Although some women needed to pay as much as $300 for each suit, the average woman spent between $800 and $1,000 on maternity clothes. Also see "Designer Diapers," *Los Angeles Times*, September 2, 1983.

39. Doris Byron Fuller, "Baby Boom Puts Style on Bottom Line," *Los Angeles Times*, September 8, 1983.

Chapter 7

1. *Los Angeles Times*, January 23, 1981.

2. *Los Angeles Times*, July 9, 1981.

3. Jody Jacobs, "First Lady Accepts Scopus Award," *Los Angeles Times*, November 17, 1981; American Presidency Project. In this announcement Elsie's birth date was given as July 22, 1919. She was still concealing her true age.

4. Pat Kivesty, "Page Boy Maternity: The Ladies and the Label," *WWD*, March 20, 1984.

5. Jennifer Seder, "Baby Boomers Usher in Whole New Concept in Maternity Wear," *Los Angeles Times*, February 8, 1985.

6. Jennifer Seder, "Sexy and Chic Are Choice Looks for the Boomlet Mother-To Be," *Los Angeles Times*, January 24, 1986.

7. See Page Boy brochures.

8. Stacy Meier, "Faces," DMN, December 8, 1985.

9. Pat Kivestu, "The Ladies and the Label," *Women's Wear Daily*, March 20, 1984.

10. Leslie Watts, "Expecting and Elegant: Maternity Fashion More Sophisticated, Varied Than in Past," *Houston Chronicle*, August 11, 1988.

11. *Park Cities People*, September 24, 1987.

12. *Park Cities People*, August 31, 1989.

13. Information from Page Boy catalogs from 1986, 1989, and 1990.

14. This statement indicates that most of Page Boy's garments were still made in the United States.

15. *Doylestown Pennsylvania Intelligencer*, April 21, 1991.

16. One wonders whether such designs had Elsie's input or approval. This description of the current styles seems far from Elsie's ideas of smart style.

17. A collective list of celebrities who wore Page Boy clothes and had their names attached to either advertisements or published articles includes: Kim Alexis, Lucille Ball, Joan Bennett, Ann Blythe, Natalie Cole, Mrs. Ronald Coleman, Jeanne Crain, Sandra Dee, Jill Eikenberry, Alice Faye, Judy Garland, Mitzi Green, Julie Harris, Florence Henderson, Gloria Henry, Mrs. Lamar Hunt, Betty Hutton, Grace Kelley, Deborah Kerr, Mrs. Alan Ladd, Mrs. Mario Lanza, Mrs. Jerry Lewis, Ali MacGraw, Dorothy Malone, Mrs. Dean Martin, Marie McDonald, Jayne Meadows, Jane Nigh,

Deborah Norville, Helen O'Connell, Jane Powell, Mrs. Hal Roach, Debby Reynolds, Gabby Rodgers (Mrs. Jerry Lieber), Roxanne (Delores Evelyn Rosedale), Barbara Rush, Dinah Shore, Maria Shriver, Jo Stafford, Barbara Streisand, Margaret Sullivan, Elizabeth Taylor, Shirley Temple, Mrs. Jack Webb, Mrs. Errol Flynn (Pat Wymore), Mary Alice Williams, Shelly Winters, Loretta Young.

18. Lisa Skolnik, "Great Expectations: Fashion Conscious Designers Deliver Offbeat Elegance to Mothers-to-Be," *Chicago Tribune,* May 1, 1991.

19. Deborah Wormser, *Dallas Morning News,* June 17, 1991.

20. Cindy LaFavre Yorks, "Fashion—Expanding the Options—Many Maternity Clothes Are Ill-Fitting and Frumpy." *Los Angeles Times,* August 9, 1991.

21. One might wonder how sophisticated or business-like baby-doll fashions actually were.

22. Lisa Skolnik, "Great Expectations."

23. Lois Cowan, telephone interview by author, July 15, 2011. Cowan also recounted a confrontation she had with Edna after her book, *Millionaires,* was published. Edna contacted her, asking whether she would write some press copy for the firm. They corresponded back and forth about what needed to be included and about the price of the work. Cowan provided Edna with the work and sent her a bill. Edna replied, saying she wanted to send her a bumblebee pin, but she never mentioned payment of the bill. Cowan said it would be nice to have the pin but pointed out that they had a contract. Eventually Cowan did get paid, but Edna never sent the pin. Cowan described Edna as manipulative and mercurial. She also described both Frankfurt sisters as driven and calculating, although Elsie covered this with softness and Southern charm while Edna masked it with eccentricity. She added that while she visited Elsie and Franklin in their home, she could see how much in love Elsie and Franklin were.

24. Penny Pollock, email dated May 16, 2011; Lois Rich-McCoy, email dated May 15, 2010. Obituary of William Campbell Lackey, *Dallas Morning News,* April 4, 2004.

25. Penny Pollock, interview with the author, September, 29, 2009.

26. Brenda Berg, interview with the author, April 14, 2010.

27. Gray, *CAD/CAM,* 5–9. Today grading a pattern only takes seconds.

28. Wausau Insurance photo album from Penny Pollock, part of the Page Boy collection belonging to Elsie Frankfurt Pollock.

29. Robert Miller, "Baylor University Institute to Honor Family-Run Businesses," *Dallas Morning News,* June 9, 1993.

30. Ammenheuser, "Mothers Work."

31. "Mothers Work to Acquire Page Boy," *Dallas Morning News,* January 6, 1994.

32. *Dallas Morning News,* undated article.

33. See Mothers Work Inc. annual reports for 1994, 1995, and 1997. Also see Securities and Exchange Commission Form 10-K for Mothers Work for fiscal year ending September 30, 1996. Joel Thornton, Assistant Professor for University Libraries at Texas A&M University, assisted the author in obtaining these documents.

34. Most of the information in this section about Robert Pollock that was not gleaned from the newspapers came from Penny Pollock. Penny Pollock, telephone interview with the author, September, 29, 2009

35. Ammenheuser, "Mothers Work."

36. Rosenberg, *Sangers'*, 116–17. Although Rosenberg was critiquing a firm that was sold in the 1920s, his observations were still valid in 1990.

37. Chandler, *Scale and Scope*, 390.

38. Rich-McCoy, *Millionairess*, 101.

39. Judie Ashworth, email, May 20, 2010.

40. Sterlacci and Arbuckle, *Historical Dictionary*. There is also no mention of Elsie Frankfurt or Page Boy Maternity Company in *Patently Female: From AZT to TV Dinners: Stories of Women Inventors and Their Breakthrough Ideas* by Ethlie Ann Vare and Greg Ptacek, published in 2002, or in *Mothers of Invention: From the Bra to the Bomb: Forgotten Women and Their Unforgettable Ideas*, published in 1988 by the same authors.

Bibliography

Archives

Dupont Archive. Hagley Museum and Library, Wilmington, Delaware.

Frankfurt Folder. Dallas Archive, Dallas Public Library.

Look and *Life* magazine collections. Library of Congress.

Margaret Herrick Library, Beverly Hills, California.

Steve Carlin Papers and Texas Jewish Historical Association Archive. Center for American History, University of Texas at Austin.

Page Boy papers and scrapbooks. Texas Fashion Collection. University of North Texas, Denton, Texas.

Government Sources

"Buttons to Biotech: 1996 Update Report." U. S. Department of Commerce, Patent and Trademark Office, April 1998.

Twelfth Census of the United States, St. Louis Missouri, 1900.

Thirteenth Census of the United States, Athens, Texas, 1910.

Fourteenth Census of the United States, Dallas, Texas, 1920.

Fifteenth Census of the United States, Erie County, New York, 1930.

U.S. Patent number 873,167, granted to R. H. Peters, December 10, 1907.

U. S. Patent number 960,689, granted to William Padernacht, December 10, 1907.

U. S. Patent number 2,051,444, granted to Aaron Haister, August 18, 1935.

U.S. Patent number 2,085,179, granted to Samuel Badanes, June 29, 1937.

Newspapers

Amarillo (TX) *Globe*

Atlanta Constitution

Binghamton (NY) *Press*

Boston Business Journal

Business Week (New York)

Chester (PA) *News*

Chicago Daily News

Chicago Tribune

Christian Science Monitor (Boston, Massachusetts)

Daily News

Dallas Morning News

Dallas Times Herald

Doylestown Pennsylvania Intelligencer

Family Weekly

Gazette (Charleston, West Virginia)

Gettysburg Times

Houston Post

Independent (Pasadena, California)

Journal American (New York)

Lacona (NY) *Citizen*

Lima (Ohio) *Citizen*

Los Angeles Times

New York Daily News

New York Times

Palladium Times (Oswego, New York)

Park Cities People (Dallas, Texas)

The Plain Dealer (Cleveland, Ohio)

San Francisco Chronicle

San Mateo Times

Wall Street Journal (New York)

Washington Post

Western Apparel Industry

Women's Wear Daily (New York)

Emails and Interviews

Brenda Berg, daughter of Louise Frankfurt Gartner. Emails and interview of April 14, 2010.

Lois Cowan, author. Interview by author July 15, 2011.

Gigi Gartner, daughter of Louise Frankfurt Gartner. Emails beginning September, 2009.

Jane Guzman, historian and Dallas resident. Email of March 26, 2010; interview of April 2, 2010.

Louise Frankfurt Gartner. Interview by author, July 26, 2008.

Louise Frankfurt Gartner. Interview by Rosalind Benjet, January 5, 2006. Dallas Jewish Historical Society CD.

Penny Pollock, stepdaughter of Elsie Frankfurt Pollock. Interview by author, September, 29, 2009, and emails continuing through June 2011.

Rosalie Ravkind, Edna Ravkind's former daughter-in-law. Interview by author, April 30, 2010.

Joan Susman. Emails beginning April 19, 2010.

Morris D. Weiss. Emails beginning September 2009.

Ralph Zeman, Dallas garment manufacturer. Interview by author, July 25, 2008.

Books, Dissertations, Journals, and Magazines

Abramson, Martin. "The New Look in Lady Millionaires." *Good Housekeeping*, September 1967.

All Florida Weekly Magazine, March 9, 1959. Page Boy scrapbook.

American Presidency Project. "Ronald Reagan Appointments." http://www.presidency.ucsb.edu/ws/index. php.

Ammenheuser, Maura K. "Mothers Work Expecting More Growth." Shopping Centers Today online news, May 2000. http://www.icsc.org/srch/sct/sct0500/06a.php.

Amnéus, Cynthia. *A Separate Sphere: Dressmakers in Cincinnati's Golden Age, 1877–1922.* Lubbock: Texas Tech University Press, 2003.

Bailey, Rebecca Lou. "Fashion in Pregnancy: An Analysis of Selected Cultural Influences, 1850–1980." Ph.D. diss., Michigan State University, 1981.

"Battle of the Bulge." *Time,* September 6, 1948.

Baumgarten, Linda. "Dressing for Pregnancy: A Maternity Gown of 1780–1795." *Dress* 23 (1996): 15–24.

Biderman, Rose. *They Came to Stay: The Story of the Jews of Dallas, 1870–1997.* Austin, TX: Eakin Press, 2002.

Blaszczyk, Regina Lee. "Styling Synthetics: Dupont Marketing of Fabric and Fashion in Postwar America." *Business History Review* 80, no. 30 (2006): 485–528.

Chandler, Alfred. *Scale and Scope: The Dynamics of Industrial Capitalism.* Boston: Harvard University Press, 1990.

Clavert, Robert A., Arnoldo De León, and Gregg Cantrell. *The History of Texas.* 4th ed. Wheeling, IL: Harlan Davidson, 2007.

DeMoss, Dorothy. *The History of Apparel Manufacturing in Texas, 1897–1981.* New York: Garland Publishing, 1989.

Devi, Indra. *Renew Your Life through Yoga.* New York: Paperback Library, 1969.

Ebony, February 1963.

Economic Policy Institute. http://www.epi.org.

Galonoy, Terry. "The Isis of Texas." *Empire for Young Executives,* 1959.

Goldman, Marilyn Kay. "Jewish Fringes, Texas Fabric: Nineteenth-Century Jewish Merchants Living Texas Reality and Myth." Ph.D. diss., Texas A&M University, 2003.

Gray, Stephen. *CAD/CAM in Clothing and Textiles.* Hampshire, UK: Gower Publishing, 1998.

Gross, L. "Self-Made Woman." *Look,* February 14, 1961.

Handbook of Texas Online. http://www.tshaonline.org/handbook/online/articles/DD/hdd1.html.

Heath, Jim F. "American War Mobilization and the Use of Small Manufacturers, 1939–1943." *The Business History Review,* 46, Number no. 3 (Autumn 1972): 295–319.

Johnson, Sarah. "The Business of Fashion: A Social History." *American Quarterly* 54 (September 2002): 467–83.

"Maternity-Dress Millions." *Enterprise: The Magazine of the Young Presidents' Organization,* January 1958.

Media Storehouse. http://www.mediastorehouse.com/pictures_618148/REAGAN-CHESTERFIELD.

Meyerowitz, Joanne. " Beyond the Feminine Mystique: A Reassessment of Postwar Mass Culture, 1946–1958." *Journal of American History,* March 1993.

Mitchell, William E., and Marshall Sklare, *Mishpokhe: A Study of New York City Jewish Family Clubs.* The Hague, Netherlands: Mouton, 1978.

Nenadic, Stana. "The Social Shaping of Business Behavior in the Nineteenth-Century Women's Garment Trade." *Journal of Social History* 31 (Spring 1998): 625–45.

Newsweek, September 13, 1948.

New Yorker, November 18, 1961.

Nolan, Carol. "Women's Fashion History." http://www.lindyhopping.com/fashionhist.html.

Peiss, Kathy. "Vital Industry and Women's Ventures: Conceptualizing Gender in Twentieth Century Business History." *Business History Review* 72 (Summer 1998): 218–41.

Poli, Doretta Davanzo. *The Twentieth Century's Histories of Fashion: Maternity Fashions.* Edited by Ieri Attualità. Modena, Italy: Zanfi Editori, 1996.

Rich-McCoy, Lois. *Millionairess: Self-Made Women of America.* New York: Harper & Roe, 1989.

Rosenberg, Leon Joseph. *Sangers': Pioneer Texas Merchants.* Austin: Texas State Historical Association Press, 1978.

Smithsonian Institution Online. "First Lady of Retailing."

http://amhistory.si.edu/archives/WIB-tour/main-Movie.html.

Sterlacci, Francesca, and Joanne Arbuckle. *Historical Dictionary of the Fashion Industry.* Lanham, MD: Scarecrow Press, 2008.

Tolbert, Frank X. *Neiman-Marcus, Texas: The Story of the Proud Dallas Store.* New York: Henry Holt, 1953.

Troxell, Mary D. *Fashion Merchandising.* New York: Gregg Division McGraw-Hill, 1976.

Walker, Nancy A. ed., *Women's Magazines, 1940–1960: Gender Roles and the Population.* Boston: Bedford/St. Martin, 1998.

Weiner, Lynn Y. *From Working Girl to Working Mother: The Female Labor Force in the United States, 1820–1980.* Chapel Hill: University of North Carolina Press, 1985.

Western Apparel: Industry, Business Magazine of the Needlecraft, October 1962.

"When a Designer Has a Baby." *Good Housekeeping,* July 1951.

Winegarten, Ruthe, and Cathy Schechter. *Deep in the Heart: The Lives and Legends of Texas Jews.* Austin, Texas: Eakin Press, 1990.

Worden, Helen. "Maternity Can Be Chic, My Dear." *Collier's,* March 25, 1950.

"Yoga on Company Time." *Life,* February 14, 1964.

Index

About the Author

Kay Goldman's research centers on Jewish business people in Texas and their relationship with the surrounding culture. She has also researched The National Council of Jewish Women in Louisiana and Texas. She lives in College Station, Texas.

Lou Halsell Rodenberger Prize

Dressing Modern Maternity is the inaugural winner of the Lou Halsell Rodenberger Prize in History and Literature. The competition is supported generously by donation. Texas Tech University Press and the author are grateful to all donors whose support made this publication possible.